Understanding the sentencing of women

edited by
Carol Hedderman and Loraine Gelsthorpe

A Research and Statistics Directorate Report

Home Office
Research and
Statistics
Directorate

London: Home Office

Home Office Research Studies

The Home Office Research Studies are reports on research undertaken by or on behalf of the Home Office. They cover the range of subjects for which the Home Secretary has responsibility. Titles in the series are listed at the back of this report (copies are available from the address on the back cover). Other publications produced by the Research and Statistics Directorate include Research Findings, the Research Bulletin, Statistical Bulletins and Statistical Papers.

The Research and Statistics Directorate

The Directorate consists of three Units which deal with research and statistics on Crime and Criminal Justice, Offenders and Corrections, Immigration and General Matters; the Programme Development Unit; the Economics Unit; and the Operational Research Unit.

 The Research and Statistics Directorate is an integral part of the Home Office, serving the Ministers and the department itself, its services, Parliament and the public through research, development and statistics. Information and knowledge from these sources informs policy development and the management of programmes; their dissemination improves wider public understanding of matters of Home Office concern.

First published 1997

Application for reproduction should be made to the Information and Publications Group, Room 201, Home Office, 50 Queen Anne's Gate, London SW1H 9AT.

©Crown copyright 1997 ISBN 1 85893 893 7
ISSN 0072 6435

Foreword

Despite frequently voiced concerns about discrimination in the criminal justice system there has been surprisingly little new research during the last decade into the way women are sentenced. The two projects described in this report seek to fill that gap: Part I examines statistical data on more than 13,000 men and women offenders; and Part II looks at the factors sentencers identify as influences on their decision-making.

While the results suggest that the way women and men are sentenced differs, it would be inaccurate and unhelpful to see this in terms of deliberate discrimination. The findings do not point to any simple formulae which can be used to ensure that both sexes receive fair treatment, but the report ends with suggestions on how we can move in that direction.

CHRIS LEWIS
Head of Offenders and Corrections Unit
Research and Statistics Directorate
June 1997

Acknowledgements

Lizanne Dowds would like to thank Brian Caraher, Pat Dowdeswell, Mark Greenhorn and Peter Marshall for their help and Carol Hedderman would like to thank Darren Sugg for his work on the matching exercise described in Part I.

Loraine Gelsthorpe and Nancy Loucks would like to thank the Clerks to Justices, their Deputies and staff along with the magistrates in the different court areas, for kind and willing co-operation in the research. We are also grateful to a small group of Cambridge magistrates for their willingness to participate in the pilot stage of the research. Mrs Tisha Hug, Administrative Secretary at the Institute of Criminology, is deserving of our sincere thanks for her support at the Cambridge University end of things in Part II of the research. We express our thanks also to Mandie Young who patiently and efficiently helped with the transcription of interview tapes.

All four authors are grateful to Anne Worrall for her comments on an early draft and to Julie Vennard for her comments on the final report.

Contents

Summary

A superficial examination of the criminal statistics suggests that, for virtually every type of offence, women are treated more leniently than men. This report describes the results of a two-part study of the sentencing of women. In Part I, sentencing patterns are explored in more detail using samples of men and women convicted of shoplifting, violence and drug offences in 1991. The results of this analysis, which was based on more than 13,000 cases, were then used to inform Part II of the study in which magistrates were interviewed about what they thought were the main influences on their decision-making.

Part I

Statistical tests were used, first, to examine whether an offender's sex appeared to affect the likelihood of a prison sentence once criminal and sentencing history was taken into account, and then, to model the likelihood of various other sentencing outcomes. The penalties that the model *predicted* each offender would receive were compared with the *actual* sentence men and women received.

- Women shoplifters were less likely than comparable males to receive a prison sentence. They were also more likely to be sentenced to a community penalty or to be discharged. However, the results should not be interpreted as evidence of a general policy of leniency towards women shoplifters. They suggest rather that sentencers may be reluctant to fine a woman – possibly because they may be penalising her children rather than just herself. This results in many women receiving a discharge but others receiving community penalties which are rather more severe than fines.

- Men and women stood an equal chance of going to prison for a first violent offence. However among repeat offenders women were less likely to receive a custodial sentence.

- Women first offenders were significantly less likely than equivalent men to receive a prison sentence for a drug offence, but recidivists were equally likely to go to prison.

- Among first and repeat offenders, women convicted of violence and drug offences were always more likely to be discharged and men more likely to be fined. But again, this seems to be less a consequence of a policy of leniency than a reluctance to impose one particular sentence – the fine – on women.

Part II

Nearly 200 magistrates were interviewed individually or in groups at five courts using a semi structured questionnaire and a small sentencing exercise involving two stereotypical cases designed to bring out differences in their thinking about men and women offenders. These interviews, which were carried out between June and December 1995, took account of the findings in *Part I.*

- Magistrates said they found it hard to compare the way they sentenced men and women because they dealt with women offenders far less frequently. However, they broadly distinguished between 'troubled' and 'troublesome' offenders, and tended to locate most women in the former category. In part this was because women tended to be first offenders, facing less serious charges than men and because they behaved more respectfully in court. In addition, magistrates tended to ascribe different motives to them. However, even when men were stealing bacon or coffee rather than alcohol or items to sell, they rarely engaged magistrates' sympathies.

- Because they regarded women offenders as troubled, magistrates responded to their offending with measures (a discharge or probation) designed to assist them to lead law-abiding lives rather than punishing them. Fines were regarded as particularly unsuitable for women with children to care for and because they were seen as lacking 'independent means' for paying fines.

- While magistrates stressed that 'the facts' of a case were most influential, many made reference to 'common sense' or 'gut feelings' determining how they approached issues of motivation, body language or the offender's personal circumstances.

- Appearance and demeanour in the courtroom were often commented on by magistrates. Although they denied that this influenced their decision–making, their comments concerning the importance of seeing the offender in court, and anecdotes about those who behaved inappropriately, suggested that these factors were influential.

Conclusion

This study reveals major differences in the use of noncustodial penalties for men and women. Women were consistently more likely than men to be discharged even when their circumstances appeared, on the basis of the available data, entirely comparable. This may stem from the fact that sentencers were reluctant to fine women. Equally though, it appears that this reluctance may sometimes result in a woman being given a more severe noncustodial penalty. To use probation where a fine would have been appropriate is an ineffective use of resources; and skipping a step on the sentencing ladder this time round – even if this is inspired by a desire not to financially penalise a woman's family – carries the risk that it will lead to an even more severe sentence being imposed in the event of a subsequent conviction.

The results concerning the use of custody are less clear cut. Overall, they suggest that while sentencers do not inevitably reject the idea of imposing prison sentences on women, women do not stand an equal chance of custody in all circumstances.

1 Introduction

Section 95 of the 1991 Criminal Justice Act imposed a duty on the Home Secretary to publish information about sex, race and cost differences in the criminal justice system. The first 'section 95' document on sex differences, published in September 1992, summarised what was known about differences in treatment as victims, defendants, offenders and employees. Gaps in knowledge were openly acknowledged along with the need for new work aimed at filling them. The research described in this report addresses one of the questions it was not then possible to answer: do sex differences in sentencing statistics simply reflect differences in the type and number of offences for which male and female offenders[1] are convicted or something more?

Before turning to a consideration of what other authors have said about sentencing differences, it is important to make it clear from the outset that this research makes no assumptions about the extent of *real* sex differences in offending or what impact a suspect's sex has on the decision to caution, prosecute or convict.[2] Our focus is entirely on the *sentencing* decision and the factors magistrates themselves perceive as affecting it.

It is also important to note that this research is based on the idea that 'equal' treatment for men and women is a matter of approach not outcome. The underlying assumption is that fairness consists of people in similar circumstances being treated in similar ways, but it must be recognised that men and women do not necessarily appear in similar circumstances. Our aim, therefore, was to describe how magistrates set about taking account of substantive differences in men's and women's lives and *their* perceptions of 'real justice' for women. The starting point for this was some analysis of differences in sentencing patterns, the results of which were used as a basis for exploring with magistrates what influences their decision-making.

---

1   The terms *male* and *female* are used when all age groups are being discussed; *men* and *women* are used only when those under discussion are aged 21 or over.

2   Criminal statistics, across time and across different cultures, do show that an overwhelming majority of those caught and convicted for criminal acts are male (see, for example, Harvey et al., 1992). Although self-report studies suggest that official statistics may overestimate sex differences in offending, they do not contradict the idea that there is a difference (e.g., Graham and Bowling, 1995). It is also true that, in England and Wales at least, cautioning is the main disposal used for female offenders. For example, over the last three years around 60 per cent of all females found guilty or cautioned for indictable offences received a caution compared with just over a third of males (37%). However, we do not know how far this reflects differences in offending or other relevant factors, such as previous offending, or how far it shows a chivalrous or paternalistic response to female offending.

Official statistics and previous research

Sentencing statistics show large overall differences in the sheer number of males and females convicted and sentenced for criminal offences (see Table 1.1). They also show differences in the proportions receiving particular types of sentences. For example, adult women sentenced for indictable offences in 1995 were twice as likely to be discharged and to be put on probation than men, but half as likely to be given a prison sentence. Also, while the use of some sentences has declined and the use of others has increased, the ratio of males and females receiving different types of sentences has remained farily constant during the 1990s, although changes in legislation, such as the introduction of the Combination Order and restrictions on the circumstances in which custody may be suspended, make it difficult to be precise.

Table 1.1 Sentences awarded to men and women (aged 21 or over) convicted of indictable offences: 1991 and 1995

	1991			1995		
	M %	F %	Ratio	M %	F %	Ratio
Sentences						
Abs/con						
discharge	15	34	0.4	15	30	0.5
Fine	39	28	1.4	34	26	1.3
Probation order	8	17	0.5	11	20	0.55
CSO	8	4	2.0	11	7	1.6
Combination						
order	N/A	N/A	–	3	3	1.0
Suspended						
sentence	10	8	1.25	1	2	0.5
Immediate						
custody	18	6	3.0	24	10	2.4
Other	2	2	1.0	2	2	1.0
Number (000's)						
= 100%	190.1	29.2	6.5	178.4	26.8	6.7

This table is based on figures taken from Table 7.13 of the Criminal Statistics, 1991 and Table 7.11 of the Criminal Statistics, 1995.

With the exception of drug offences, sentencing statistics show overall sex differences for individual indictable offences too. Among those convicted of drug offences, men and women were equally likely to receive a CSO or an unsuspended custodial sentence (approximately 7% and 16% respectively).

As well as being generally less likely to receive a custodial sentence than men, women also tend to receive shorter terms of imprisonment: in 1995 the average length of prison sentences imposed for indictable offences at the Crown Court was 17.7 months for women aged 21 or over and 22 months for men. The average length was lower for females convicted of burglary, fraud and forgery, robbery, and theft and handling, but higher for criminal damage and drug offences.

In the 1970s and 1980s a number of British studies attempted to examine the question of why men and women appear to have such different sentencing patterns. Some of these studies (Pearson, 1976; Eaton, 1983, 1986; Edwards, 1984; Worrall, 1987, 1990) focused on interactional aspects of the magistrates' court process. They were not concerned with measuring differences between male and female defendants in terms of factors such as their past or present offending, but in how differences in the way they behaved and how they were perceived affected the decision-making process. Of particular note here is work which draws attention to the impact of appearance and demeanour in the courtroom, though as Hedderman (1990) points out, having carried out a systematic observational study in an English magistrates' court in 1985, the relationship between how magistrates appear to react to defendants and how they actually sentence people is by no means clear. Hedderman concluded that some of the differences between the sentences imposed on men and women could be accounted for by the way they behave in the courtroom, with women receiving more lenient sentences than men because they are more nervous and act more respectfully and deferentially to the court. Worrall (1990) discusses the importance of congruence between appearance, demeanour and lifestyle and apparent sexual normality in magistrates' assessments of women who merit compassion and those who do not. In contrast to these sorts of studies, studies which *did* attempt to quantify sentencing differences (but ignored interaction in the courtroom) came up with somewhat conflicting results (Young, 1979; Kapardis and Farrington, 1981; Farrington and Morris, 1983). For example, Young's study of over 2,000 court records and Kapardis and Farrington's small-scale sentencing simulation study both concluded that the defendant's sex had an independent effect on sentence when other factors were controlled, whereas Farrington and Morris's correlational analysis of 400 court records found that it did not.

Roger Hood's study (1992) is one of the few to have compared the sentencing of men and women at the Crown Court using multivariate techniques. He found that women were less likely to be sentenced to custody than men when purely legal factors were taken into account and when socio-demographic factors (e.g., unemployment) were controlled. Hood also succinctly explains why various authors, such as Seear and Player (1986), Carlen (1988) and NACRO (1991), have misinterpreted prison statistics when they argue that women are *more likely* to receive custody than men. He points out that these statistics, which show that the sentenced female prison population contains proportionately more first offenders than the male population, are an inappropriate basis from which to draw conclusions about sentencing as they concern those *in prison*, not those being *imprisoned*. In fact, more recently, analysis of an Offenders Index sample of 21,000 offenders convicted of a serious offence in 1991 showed that women first offenders were half as likely to be given a sentence of immediate custody as male first offenders –4% compared with 8 per cent. Those with previous convictions were also less likely to go to prison than equivalent men (Hedderman and Hough, 1994).

In the United States, Kathleen Daly (1994) has recently attempted to combine both statistical analysis and more qualitative information from transcripts and pre-sentence investigation reports concerning those cases. She first collected information on a sample of routine cases (397) dealt with in a New Haven felony court between July 1981 and July 1986 and then more detailed information on 40 matched pairs of men and women from within this wide sample. With knowledge of the biographies of the convicted men and women, the character of their lawbreaking, and the justifications of court officials for punishment, Daly shows that sentencing disparity is negligible in the matched (deep) sample; in other words, men and women were not sentenced differently for like crimes. But another of Daly's most significant findings is the complexity of decision-making in the courtroom and the need to combine statistical analyses with qualitative data in order to gain a proper understanding of the processes of decision-making.

Methodology

This report describes the results of a two-part study of sentencing practice in England and Wales which focuses on explaining why men and women's sentencing patterns are so different. Part I adopted a purely quantitative approach using data derived from the Offenders Index and a small amount of additional data on a matched subsample of cases.

The Home Office Offender's Index is a criminal history database, containing information on around six million offenders convicted of serious (Standard List) offences. This information includes the offender's name, date of birth, date of conviction, number and nature of current and previous convictions, and current and previous sentences. For new cases since 1991, it also contains information on the offender's ethnic status.

Three samples of adult offenders were drawn from the OI for six weeks in 1991:

- 3,763 shoplifters (i.e. convicted of 'theft from shops')

- 6,547 violent offenders

- 3,670 drug offenders.

These three offence types were chosen because they were thought to reflect different perceptions of female offenders. Shoplifting cases were chosen because this is usually portrayed as a 'typical' female crime (and indeed it is the most common form of female offending according to the criminal statistics). Violent offences were chosen because violence is perceived as atypical female behaviour and it has been claimed that violent women and girls are penalised for not conforming to the female stereotype as well as for their criminal acts (e.g., Datesman and Scarpetti, 1980). Finally, we examined the sentencing of drug offenders because it is the only indictable offence for which similar proportions of men and women go to prison.

The sentencing sample was taken from 1991 because we wanted to analyse sentencing patterns *before* the interviews were conducted with magistrates, so that the former could inform the latter, and, at the time this research began (1994), more recent data was unavailable on the OI. As Table 1 1 indicates, there is little reason to assume that analysing a more recent sample of cases would yield very different results.

A variety of techniques (see Appendix A) were used to examine the sentencing of these three sets of offenders with a view to discovering whether various sentence types were used differently for comparable men and women; and, if so, what factors might affect this.

In Part II, 189 lay magistrates and eight stipendiary magistrates were interviewed during the second half of 1995 about how they approached the sentencing decision and what factors most influenced their decisions. In particular, those interviewed were asked whether they would treat men and women differently if they appeared for theft, drug or violent offences. Among the other topics covered were magistrates' backgrounds, the extent and sort of training they had received, the impact of recent legislation on their sentencing decisions, and the role of psychiatric and pre-sentence reports The five courts from which interviewees were drawn were chosen because they had been shown to be particularly harsh or lenient to one sex in Part I. The sample involved 94 female and 103 male magistrates with roughly equal proportions of men and women being interviewed in each court. Seventy-three magistrates were interviewed individually and the remainder were interviewed in 23 groups. This combination made it possible to learn about how individual magistrates formed impressions about defendants and, by observing the group dynamics, to draw some (tentative) conclusions about the dynamics of interaction on the bench. Interviews were semi-structured and included a discussion of a specific case drawn from real life involving either a male or female offender (see Appendix C).

Outline of the report

Chapter 2 describes the results of the analyses carried out in Part I of the study and discusses what they reveal about sex differences in sentencing. In Chapter 3 we turn to Part II of the study and consider some of the key points magistrates made in interview about the way in which they go about decision-making and what they see as influencing their decision–making. Chapter 4 describes how magistrates use information about offenders' personal circumstances. In the final chapter of the report (Chapter 5) we draw together the main findings of both parts of the study and consider how far these add to our understanding of the sentencing of women.

Part I:
The sentencing of men and women

Lizanne Dowds and Carol Hedderman

2 Part 1:- Looking for 'leniency' and explaining difference

What is leniency?

Although we no longer speak of a sentencing 'tariff' (Wasik, 1993), sentencers, offenders and the public inevitably rank sentences in terms of severity: (usually) from discharges through fines and to community service orders, with imprisonment as the most severe penalty our law allows. It is less easy to see how probation and suspended sentences fit into this hierarchy, partly because their actual impact may differ from the intended one. For example, a sentencer may impose a probation order because an offender cannot pay a fine, but the offender may see probation as more stigmatising and intrusive. At the other extreme, a suspended sentence imposed so that the offender faces the prospect of immediate custody if he or she reoffends, may be perceived by the offender as equivalent to a conditional discharge unless (or until) a further offence is committed.

The difficulties involved in ordering the sentences in between discharges and imprisonment partly explain why so many studies have focused on the decision to use custody. It is also, technically, the first decision that the sentencer must make:

> '..it is an approach which reflects the principle contained in s.22(2) of the Powers of the Criminal Court Act 1973 that the sentencer should first consider whether a custodial sentence would be appropriate in the absence of power to suspend.' (Moxon, 1988: 5).

Kapardis and Farrington (1981) dealt with the problem of comparative sentence severity by asking magistrates themselves to rank a series of different sentences and then used the resulting scale in their subsequent analyses.

The problem with this approach is that it reinforces the notion that differences in the sentencing on men and women are simply a matter of

9

'leniency' or 'severity', and fails to question why some forms of noncustodial penalties are used more often for men, and others are used more often for women. Losing the categorical nature of the outcomes may streamline the analysis but it may also portray the sentencing decision as one point on a one-dimensional continuum.

The current study also makes use of a very simple ranking system in which a fine is deemed to be the next most 'lenient' sentence after a discharge. Probation is regarded as more severe than a fine because, while fines are awarded for (trivial) motoring offences, probation is intended to constrain and reform those who show a more persistent tendency to offend. It is also appropriate that probation should not be treated as a punishment of first resort because of cost (currently around £2,300 per order per year), whereas a fine can actually generate revenue.[1] The suspended sentence, because of its custodial potential, is viewed as a severe penalty which is at least equivalent to a CSO.[2] Although we did not assume that sentencers move step-by-step up and down a sentencing tariff, we employed a simple ranking system for sentences, with discharges at the most lenient end of the spectrum, then fines, probation, community service orders (CSOs), suspended sentences, and unsuspended custody. The relationship between sentence and factors such as the number and nature of current offences, age, age at first offence, number of previous offences, previous experience of custody, location and type of sentencing court and, of course, sex was then examined for first offenders and recidivists.[3] Further statistical models for each set of recidivists (and sometimes for first offenders) were then built which predict:

- prison versus other

- discharge versus fine versu other

- discharge/fine versus other community penalty versus prison.

The techniques used to develop these models are described in Appendix A.

---

1   In Kapardis and Farrington's (1981) study, magistrates judged probation to be less severe than a *heavy* fine. However, Moxon (1988) notes the efforts made to promote probation as a fairly severe disposal and points out that many more of those given probation orders (at Crown Court) in 1985 had previously served custodial sentences than was the case in 1981.
2   Combination orders were not available in 1991.
3   The term recidivist is used in this report to refer to someone whose target offence was a reconviction, although strictly speaking it means someone who has reoffended (whether or not this results in a conviction).

Theft from shops

The shoplifting sample consisted of 2,696 men and 1,067 women. Men and women were similar in that two-thirds of each group were over 25 years of age at the time of sentence and the average age of both groups was between 32 and 33. Also, four per cent of men and three per cent of women were appearing in connection with a breach of a previous court order. Aside from that the samples were quite different: only a fifth of the men were appearing for the first time, compared with two-fifths of the women; and the average number of previous offences for males was 15 compared with four for females. Also, only 10 per cent of women had previously served a custodial sentence compared with 40 per cent of men.

Overall, the sentencing pattern for men and women shoplifters was generally similar to that revealed by Criminal Statistics for all offenders. The pattern was also consistent for both first offenders and recidivists. As Table 2.1 shows, women were generally more likely than men to be discharged or given a probation order, less likely to be fined and less likely to be given a custodial sentence.

Table 2.1 Sentences received by shoplifters – first offenders and recidivists

| | First offenders | | Recidivists | |
| | Men | Women | Men | Women |
	%	%	%	%
Discharge	28	44	17	30
Fine	59	42	39	26
Probation	7	9	14	24
CSO	2	–	6	4
Suspended sentence	5	3	7	9
Prison	8	1	15	5
Total	529	422	2,167	645

First time shoplifters

In the first instance the data were analysed to discover which factors were associated with the use of custody or a discharge for all three groups of offenders. For first time shoplifters this exercise showed that men in general were more likely than women to get a custodial sentence, as were those appearing for three or more offences and those appearing at the Crown Court or dealt with by Inner London magistrates' courts.

Table 2.2 shows that sex differences in sentencing were still apparent, even when seriousness was controlled for by looking only at the most minor offences (where the offender appeared for only a single theft offence at magistrates' courts outside London).

Table 2.2 Sentences received by first offenders for the most minor shoplifting offences

	Men %	Women %
Discharge	30	43
Fine	59	48
Probation	4	7
CSO	3	–
Suspended sentence	2	1
Prison	3	–
Total	277	234

While there were few clear differences between men and women at the severe end of the sentencing scale, women were significantly less likely than men to be fined for a first conviction for shoplifting and more likely to be discharged. Whether this implies that sentencers are treating women leniently is a point returned to below.

Shoplifters with previous convictions

For shoplifters with previous convictions, use of custody was strongly related to being sentenced at the Crown Court and the number of offences dealt with at the target appearance. The number of previous convictions, time since the last court appearance, previous experience of suspended or immediate custody and a previous conviction for burglary were also important.

The final model built from the variables that were related to custody independently of each other and which best explained the sentencing decision is contained in Appendix B (Table 1). It shows that although the number of current offences, being dealt with at the Crown Court, and number of previous convictions were all more important - sex was still significantly correlated with custody even when all the other variables were taken into account. In other words, women shoplifters with previous convictions were less likely than men with previous convictions to be sentenced to prison, and this was not simply a consequence of differences in their current or previous offending, previous sentencing, or where they were sentenced. However, we also need to consider whether the sex of the offender is related to the choice among noncustodial penalties (i.e., discharges, fines, community penalties and suspended sentences).

The factors which influence the choice between noncustodial options may well be rather different from those affecting the likelihood of a prison sentence:

> *'Whereas when looking at decisions relating to custodial sentences it makes sense to think in terms of aggravating and mitigating factors, these concepts do not apply in the same way to the choice among non-custodial sentences. Whilst the gravity of the offence is always an important consideration, if an offence does not warrant custody the needs and expected response of the individual may take precedence over the need for punishment.'* (Moxon, 1988: 43)

> *'The unavailability of some penalties in some areas or for some groups may also affect the sentencing decision.'* (Hedderman and Hough, 1994)

It is certainly true that many of the factors that were strongly related to the use of custody were only weakly related to the likelihood of a discharge. To examine this further, two discriminant analyses were carried out (see Appendix A for an explanation this technique). The first modelled whether offenders would receive a discharge, a fine or a 'more severe' penalty. The second combined discharges and fines as 'less severe' and sought to predict whether offenders would receive this, a 'more severe' but noncustodial penalty, or custody.

Perhaps the most notable aspects of these results are the discrepancies between what was predicted and the actual sentence for men and women (see Table 2.3). Nearly half of the male shoplifters for whom the model predicted a discharge were fined, whereas 52% of the women were discharged as predicted. However, when the model wrongly predicted a woman would receive a discharge, she was as likely to receive a more severe penalty (usually probation) as a fine.

Table 2.3 Percentage of predicted sentences which proved correct for shoplifters (I)

	Predicted Sentence					
	Discharge		Fine		Other more severe	
	Men	Women	Men	Women	Men	Women
	%	%	%	%	%	%
Actual Sentence						
Discharge	**35**	**52**	25	35	11	21
Fine	48	25	**54**	**36**	18	15
Other more severe	17	23	21	29	**71**	**65**
N	52	61	1,181	305	931	278

The majority of men for whom the model predicted a fine, were fined, but women were just as likely to receive a discharge as a fine and almost as likely to receive a more severe penalty. One explanation of this may be that sentencers are reluctant to fine women, opting for a discharge in some cases but also using more severe community penalties than they would for a comparable man.

Table 2.4 shows how actual and predicted sentencing matched up when fines and discharges were combined, community penalties formed a middle category, and prison sentences were included as the most severe option. This model, like the previous one, showed that no matter what was predicted women were always less likely than men to be given custody, and to receive a community penalty. The difference between the proportions of men and women receiving a community penalty was also rather too great to be explained just by a reluctance to send women to prison.

Table 2.4 Percentage of predicted sentences which proved correct for shoplifters (II)

Actual Sentence	Predicted sentence					
	Fine or discharge		'Severe' noncustodial		Prison	
	Men	Women	Men	Women	Men	Women
	%	%	%	%	%	%
Discharge or fine	75	69	28	29	10	7
'Severe' noncustodial	20	30	47	60	35	64
Prison	5	1	24	12	54	29
N	1,465	463	467	139	232	42

Violent offences

Of the 6,547 violent offenders in the study, 450 were women and 6,097 were men. The average age for both men and women was 30, with around 60 per cent of both groups being over the age of 25. Fifty six per cent of the women were appearing for the first time (double the proportion of men) and only eight per cent had experienced a custodial sentence before, compared with 23 per cent of men. The average number of previous offences was three for women as opposed to eight for men.

Previous research has shown that compensation is much more likely for violent offences, where there is an identifiable victim, than for shoplifting offences where – if the offender has been caught the property may well have been recovered (Moxon et al. 1992). Table 2.5 shows that, like shoplifters, women convicted of violent offences were less likely than comparable men to be given a prison sentence, community service or a fine and were more likely to be put on probation or discharged.

Table 2.5 Sentences received by violent offenders – first offenders and recidivists

| | First offenders | | Recidivists | |
| | Men | Women | Men | Women |
	%	%	%	%
Compensation	4	6	3	6
Discharge alone	28	48	16	28
Fine	37	18	27	15
Probation	4	10	9	21
CSO	5	2	7	6
Suspended Sentence	11	8	13	14
Prison	12	8	25	10
Total N (=100%)	1,685	252	4,412	198
of which (%) Fines, discharges with compensation and compensation alone	51	46	36	32

The importance of compensation orders goes beyond the fact that they are occasionally used as the sole disposal for violent offenders. If sentencers see women as less able than men to pay fines they may seek alternative disposals wherever possible (hence the high use of discharges and community penalties); but if the same sentencers are under pressure to award compensation they may feel obliged to impose that form of monetary penalty at least. It may also be that this extra element of punishment obviates the need for a more severe penalty when a discharge is simply not enough. Certainly sentencers are very strongly encouraged to award compensation wherever possible. According to the 1982 Criminal Justice Act, compensation takes precedence over a fine where the offender lacks the means to pay both - if necessary the fine should be reduced or not imposed at all (Moxon et al. 1992).

Table 2.5 shows that disparities in the way men and women are sentenced are greatly reduced if sentences which have some sort of financial element are considered together. Whether there is a corresponding reduction in the apparent use of 'harsher' punishments for women who are not fined is returned to below.

First-time violent offenders

Initial analyses showed no significant difference in the likelihood of first-time male and female violent offenders being sentenced to custody. Being dealt with at the Crown Court was the best predictor of a custodial sentence for violent offenders. In fact, exactly three per cent of men and three per cent of women were given custody at magistrates' courts (where the majority of these cases were heard).

The lack of a sex difference here is interesting – given that previous analyses (and most subsequent ones) show a tendency against the imprisonment of women. A closer examination of individual cases show that women were disproportionately likely to appear on charges of cruelty to children. Such cases seem to have been taken very seriously by the courts and when found guilty both men and women were fairly likely to receive prison sentences. But even when these cases are excluded from the analysis there was still no significant difference between the likelihood of men and women receiving a custodial sentence.

Violent offenders with previous convictions

The picture is quite different for violent offenders with previous convictions where women were significantly less likely to receive custodial sentences when other potential influences were taken into account. Also associated with using custody were: being dealt with at the Crown Court, being dealt with for a serious offence, being dealt with for more than one offence, having an extensive criminal record and previous experience of custody (see Appendix B, Table 2).

In order to look at patterns in sentencing, once the use of custody was excluded, several further analyses were carried out. First, discharges/fines and compensation orders alone were combined as the 'least serious' option against 'severe' noncustodial sentences (community penalties and suspended sentences) and custody. Again, it is the discrepancies between the predicted and the actual values that are of most interest (Table 2.6).

Table 2.6 Percentage of predicted sentences which proved correct for violent offenders (I)

	Discharge		Fine		Prison	
	Predicted Sentence					
	Men	Women	Men	Women	Men	Women
Actual Sentence	%	%	%	%	%	%
Discharge/fine/ comp	74	73	22	28	5	5
Severe noncustodial	21	23	50	63	33	65
Prison	5	4	28	9	63	30
N	2,415	112	753	46	1,243	40

The results show that no matter what is predicted women were less likely than men to receive a custodial sentence; and that they were more likely to receive a community penalty. Further analyses, in which discharges and fines were examined separately, also showed that only 31 per cent of women for whom a fine was predicted received one, with 48 per cent being discharged, whereas 50 per cent of men for whom a fine was predicted received one and only 28 per cent received a discharge instead. From this it is clear that violent women who escape a fine are no more likely than men to receive a more severe sentence.

Drug offences

The drug offender sample consisted of 3,338 men and 332 women. Once again there was no significant difference in average age which was 29 for men and 30 for women (although 63% of the women were over 25 compared with only 53% of the men). Women were much more likely to be first offenders (53% vs 25%) and the average number of their previous offences was also lower – three offences, as opposed to nine for men. They were also less likely to have experienced a custodial sentence on a previous occasion (9% vs 27%).

Criminal statistics show that about equal numbers of men and women drug offenders receive custodial sentences. In the current sample a somewhat higher proportion of men than women were sentenced to prison. This is because young offenders were excluded from the analysis.[4] Table 2.7 shows the sentences given for first offenders and recidivists.

Table 2.7 Sentences received by drug offenders – first offenders and recidivists

	First offenders		Recidivists	
	Men	Women	Men	Women
	%	%	%	%
Discharge	12	28	10	25
Fine	58	42	52	30
Probation	2	16	6	21
CSO	3	1	4	2
Suspended sententence	6	8	7	8
Prison	19	15	20	15
Total	819	177	2,519	155

For first offenders the results of the initial analysis proved unexpected in that *sex* was not significantly associated with the use of custody, while other variables showed very strong relationships indeed. Older defendants, those appearing for a serious drugs offence (supplying or manufacturing rather than just possession), and those appearing at the Crown Court were all more likely to receive a prison sentence. However, the profile of men and women defendants was rather curious in the case of drug offences. For both the other offences examined here, women tended on the whole to have a markedly less serious criminal history and to be involved in more minor cases in general – this is consistent with much of what is known about the patterns of offending among women. But women drug offenders did tend to appear a little more 'deviant' than usual. Women who were first-time drug offenders were older than their male counterparts, they were also somewhat more likely to be charged with a serious drug offence and more likely than men to be dealt with at the Crown Court. Women drug offenders with previous convictions also tended to be older than their male counterparts, they were more likely than men to have a history of fraud and forgery, to have had at least one previous probation order, and they were slightly more likely to have been charged with several offences (though they were not more likely to be dealt with at the Crown Court or to be facing more serious

---

4   When 17- to 21-year-olds year olds were included, 15% of males and 14% of females convicted of drug offences were sentenced to custody.

charges). The most likely explanation for this is that such offenders were 'drug mules' i.e., foreign nationals convicted of trafficking offences.[5]

When the use of custody for first-time drug offenders was modelled, women were less likely to receive a custodial sentence when all the other variables were taken into account (see Appendix B, Table 3). However, women recidivists were as likely as men to receive a custodial sentence.

Factors influencing the likelihood of being discharged for a drugs offence are clear-cut. The *only* factors which were significantly associated with getting a discharge on a first appearance were the defendant's sex, whether the case was heard at a magistrates' court or the Crown Court, and the seriousness of the offence. For recidivists the picture was similar. The main things that appeared to matter were (again) sex, type of court and offence seriousness. However, the number of current offences and whether the offender was in breach of a court order were also important. On the whole, the criminal and sentencing history of the defendant appeared to be unrelated to the likelihood of getting a discharge.

Table 2.8 Percentage of predicted sentences which proved correct for drug offenders (I)

| | Predicted sentence | | | |
| | Fine | | More severe sentence | |
	Men %	Women %	Men %	Women %
Actual Sentence				
Discharge	13	32	5	13
Fine	**75**	46	12	7
More severe	12	22	**83**	**81**
N	1,608	93	911	62

Table 2.8 shows that again women are always more likely to get a discharge and men are more likely to get a fine – no matter what is predicted. But when a fine is predicted and not given, women are more likely than men to end up with a harsher penalty. Women are just as likely as men to get a severe penalty when one is predicted – but when the sentencer rejects a severe penalty women tend to be discharged and men fined. These results are consistent with the theory that sentencers are reluctant to fine women.

5   Green et al. (1994) found that 87% (N=144) of the women drug 'mules' in their study of offenders sentenced for illegal drug importation were given custodial sentences compared to 78% (N=316) of the male couriers.

Conclusions

The results reported in this chapter raise as many questions as they answer. There is certainly a *tendency* towards less use of custody for women offenders – but it is equally true that sometimes there is no difference in the treatment of men and women offenders. And why should women who are first-time violent offenders or recidivist drug offenders be treated no differently from their male counterparts while sentencers appear to avoid custodial sentences for the other groups of women?

Certainly it is not possible to explain this by positing a simple, direct relationship between the type of offence for which a woman is convicted and how she is perceived. Data on the seriousness of the offence and the remand status of the defendants may help to explain this further, but the safest conclusion (from this data) concerning the use of custody is that it is often but not always the case that women are less likely than men to be given a prison sentence.

However although the whole sentencing debate (perhaps inevitably) tends to focus around use of custody, this analysis shows that major discrepancies between the sentencing of men and women lie in the choice between noncustodial options. Women were consistently more likely than men to be discharged even when their circumstances appeared (on the basis of the available data) entirely comparable. This may stem from the fact that sentencers were (for whatever reason) reluctant to fine women. Equally though, it appears that this reluctance to fine women may sometimes result in a woman being given a more severe noncustodial penalty. Thus, this phase of the study shows different women being treated more leniently *and* more harshly. This leaves us with a number of questions: why are sentencers reluctant to fine women? Is it because they are reluctant to penalise the whole family for her misdemeanour if she is not working and her husband/partner provides the money for the household? Does this not also apply to men in similar circumstances – or is it that the results show up for women offenders simply because more of them are in this situation, as Farrington and Morris (1983) suggest.[6]

In order to begin to resolve some of these questions, we extracted a sub-sample of magistrates' court cases involving men and women (N=363) matched on age, criminal history, offence and plea. We then asked the sentencing courts to provide information on whether the offender had been remanded in custody prior to sentence and details of their marital and economic status. Because the cases were sentenced in 1991, it was only

---

6   Farrington and Morris found that 'current problems' (including financial ones) was one of the main predictors of a more lenient sentence, and there was no difference between the sentences men and women received once this was taken into account.

possible to obtain full information in a small number of cases.

The questionnaire was returned for 137 pairs of offenders (an overall response of 37%) but even in these cases there was often missing information.[7] So while it is noteworthy that married and single women were equally likely to be fined but married men were twice as likely to be fined than unmarried ones, one cannot draw any firm conclusions from this. Similarly, the fact that fines were given to 70 per cent of employed men versus 57 per cent of employed women and equal proportions of the unemployed were fined (40%) is interesting but inconclusive because of the numbers involved. However, even if this difference was found to be inspired by a desire not to financially penalise a woman's family, it carries the risk that, skipping a step on the sentencing ladder this time round, will lead to an even more severe sentence being imposed in the event of a subsequent conviction. To use probation where a fine would have been appropriate is also an ineffective use of resources (Moxon et al., 1990).

As 96 per cent of men and women were bailed, we can say little about the impact custodial remands have on sentencing from this exercise, except that as half the matched pairs who were bailed and half of those remanded in custody were given the same disposal, and the others were given different ones, it seems unlikely that remand status had much impact on the sentencing decision.

In the next section of this report Loraine Gelsthorpe and Nancy Loucks explore whether magistrates believe these factors should and do influence their decision-making and what other considerations affect their sentencing choices for men and women offenders.

---

7   Information on marital status was available on 96 offenders, employment status for 136 offenders and remand status for 206 offenders.

Part II:
Magistrates' explanations of sentencing decisions

Loraine Gelsthorpe and Nancy Loucks

3 Part II:- Justice in the making: key influences on decision-making[1]

Magistrates are supposed to have a certain degree of intelligence – certainly stipendiaries are – and an ability to assess human beings and the manner in which they give their evidence and the way that they come over and behave themselves, and conduct themselves. Stipe. at one of the sample courts (M)[2]

There's still something of the defence for sex, I'm afraid. And you really wonder how the innocent-looking young lady in front of you, who's obviously been told by her solicitor to look as helpless as possible, could possibly have undertaken the violent elements that are there. Mag. 3, Hallam court (M)

In this part of the study 189 lay and eight stipendiary magistrates were interviewed either in groups or individually. From these discussions it emerged that magistrates saw offenders broadly in terms of whether they were primarily 'troubled' or 'troublesome'; and the group an offender fell into was determined by factors such as motive for the offence, degree of provocation, relationship to victim, abuse of drugs or alcohol, and mental state. It was also affected by the way an offender behaved in court, by the way magistrates perceived other courtroom 'players' and the information they provided, and by magistrates' awareness of how their decisions might be seen by others. Together these factors shaped magistrates' views of an appropriate sentence.

---

1 The following two chapters describe the main results of research by Loraine Gelsthorpe and Nancy Loucks. A fuller discussion "The Remanding and Sentencing of Women Offenders in Magistrates' courts: views from the bench" will be published shortly.

2 We assigned a number to each magistrate we interviewed to ensure anonymity and confidentiality. For the same reason, individual courts are not identified when quoting the views of a Chairman of the Bench or a Stipendiary magistrate. The 'M' or 'F' designates each magistrate as male or female.

Images of offenders: troubled or troublesome?

Think of them as greedy, needy or dotty. Group 3, Shelley court (F)

One explanation which magistrates gave for differences in the sentences given to men and women was that their motives were rarely similar. In their opinion, a 'typical' shop theft committed by a female defendant differed considerably from the 'typical' thefts which men committed:

> *...the women feed the family whereas the men, although they have to support their family, don't.* Mag. 13, Byron court (F)

'Troubled' offenders include those who steal items from shops which they, or particularly their children, need (mainly food, or sometimes clothing or shoes, but nothing very extravagant). This definition stretches to women (specifically) who steal tins of salmon, for example, as a treat for the family which they otherwise could not afford. Indeed, magistrates described this as the most typical scenario they dealt with when sentencing women convicted of shop theft. In contrast, those interviewed portrayed men as stealing out of greed rather than need:

> *...a shoplifting woman would probably be a single mother without enough money. A shoplifting man would very rarely be a single father without enough money and kids yapping around – they would be lads out on the town wanting to get a snappy pair of jeans...* Mag. 12, Shelley court (F)

Rather than food or shoes, men were characterised as stealing alcohol or CDs and videos to sell. Magistrates commonly referred to women as stealing to feed their children where men stole to support drug habits. Even offences relating to prostitution could often fall into this 'survival' category. Some magistrates viewed it as something which was legally an offence, but which did little harm.

To some extent, fraud against the Department of Social Security was also seen as being for 'survival'. Magistrates generally sympathised with women who 'did a couple of cleaning jobs on the side every once in a while' and 'didn't realise' that they were doing something wrong, or had become dependent on the extra income. Men were invariably seen as much more deliberate and profit-driven.

Although this was exceptional, women could be 'troublesome' rather than 'troubled'. Magistrates expressed least tolerance for women shoplifters whose offences were planned and/or done for profit – in other words, those whose offences were closer to the stereotype of the male shoplifter. They said that such women tended to work in groups and 'stole to order'. Some women were even believed to use their children either as a distraction or trained them to take the goods themselves (though magistrates thought that this was relatively infrequent).

Surprisingly perhaps, some violent offences were viewed by magistrates with a degree of understanding. To draw out the reasons for this, interviewees were asked to consider a real, but anonymised, case involving an assault by a female (see Appendix C). In this case, 'Jane' attacked her husband's lover. Magistrates usually believed that Jane had been provoked and that the victim probably deserved what she got (to the extent that some magistrates did not think it was appropriate to award compensation).

Interestingly, a third (N=12) of the individual magistrates and a quarter of the groups (N=3) who were asked about this case vignette found her behaviour 'understandable' and several commented that they might well have done the same thing in her situation. On the other hand, magistrates who were asked to look at details of a case involving a man, 'Jason', who assaulted a man who made an obscene gesture at Jason's friend in a motoring dispute (see Appendix C), had little sympathy with him. Only four individual magistrates out of 28 and one group out of the 12 who looked at this case study could see any element of provocation.

One magistrate explained that where women commit violent offences, they tend to commit offences against people they know (an abusive partner, perhaps, or a neighbour or friend), with some identifiable cause. Men, on the other hand, are apt to be involved in offences against strangers, such as in pub brawls. These too may have an identifiable cause, but such causes tend to be unrelated to the victims of the offence. Examples those interviewed gave included expressions of frustration because of offenders' redundancy or continued unemployment, or their consumption of alcohol or drugs. This could explain some of the differences in sentencing identified in Part I.

Factors relating to family background, such as a history of abuse during childhood, met with a mixed reception. Forty-six individual magistrates and 10 groups who mentioned such factors said they would take them into consideration. Fifteen individuals and three groups specifically said they would not; and nine individual and 10 groups of magistrates had no clear view on this matter.

While a small number of magistrates (four out of the eight who mentioned it) believed that male and female co-defendants would be regarded as equally culpable, others (three individuals and one group) commented that they were inclined to believe that a woman invariably played a lesser role or was perhaps coerced into committing an offence rather than sharing equal responsibility:

> *If a man and a woman come up together, there will be a tendency, unless you were told otherwise, [to assume] that the man was influencing the woman, that the man was the ringleader. This happens with juveniles, that a younger juvenile is influenced by the older juvenile... I think that is ingrained, a man and a woman together that you are expecting the man to be dominant.* Mag. 10, Byron (M)

> *...there is a tendency to feel that women are more victims than men in that they are more vulnerable, the pressures of their various partners, and that they are following rather than instigating.* Mag. 14, Byron (F)

Ten individual magistrates and two groups also mentioned that they believed male offenders used women in crimes – to steal pension books or pass stolen cheques for example – in the belief that, if caught, they would be dealt with more leniently. Interestingly, one magistrate commented that male offenders would never admit to being led by a woman, with the result that, at most, female co-defendants would share equal blame and probably much less. This in turn may produce disparity in the sentencing of men and women facing the same charge.

Magistrates expressed a general lack of tolerance of addiction to drugs or alcohol, which they viewed as self-inflicted problems. In addition only one group distinguished between binge drinking (which few would dispute is a matter of choice) and addiction (which is treated by the medical profession as an illness). Although magistrates said that they quite frequently recommended drug or alcohol programmes (16 individual magistrates and four groups mentioned this specifically), to some extent they viewed such programmes as an 'easy option'. Two magistrates also said that they would refer defendants to such programmes only once, after which they considered a more punitive response appropriate.

Magistrates very rarely viewed intoxication as a mitigating factor. Only one magistrate mentioned this possibility, whereas eight individuals and four groups were clear that it would *not* mitigate. In fact, eight individual magistrates and six groups thought that intoxication could well have an aggravating effect on sentence.

Drugs-related crime was generally viewed very seriously by the magistrates. Only possession of drugs for one's own consumption (with no other connected offences) was thought to warrant anything other than a very severe response. Few magistrates reported having any direct experience of sentencing women for dealing in drugs or even for possession. The main exception seemed to be women who resorted to prostitution to feed a drugs habit. This tended to be viewed as 'hurting no-one but themselves'. In contrast, men were characterised as likely to resort to burglary to feed a drug habit. If women were involved in selling drugs at all, then the magistrates believed that men were usually behind it (e.g., as pimps or suppliers).

Proof of some form of mental illness, on the other hand, was an acceptable form of mitigation. A further factor mentioned was 'hormonal problems' for older women. Male magistrates in particular tended to mention 'the Change' as an explanation of offending, especially shop theft. Only one female magistrate introduced this idea among the six individuals and four groups who mentioned it. Again, this perceived 'illness' generated sympathy rather than censure.

Magistrates' impression that most of those charged with not having a TV licence are women is confirmed by the sentencing statistics. All those interviewed described this offence as deserving of compassion. Magistrates believed that these women were doing their best in a bad situation: they could not afford their licence, or their husbands would not give them the money for it. Single mothers were particularly vulnerable as they relied heavily on the television to occupy their children. Magistrates also recognised that where women lived with partners, they were the ones who were most likely to answer the door while their children were watching the television (and thus they were the ones charged with having no TV licence).

In contrast there were a few particular offences which individual magistrates and groups said they could not understand and offenders with whom they could never empathise. The most commonly mentioned of these was having no motor insurance (mentioned by four individuals and three groups) – an almost entirely male offence in the view of those whom we interviewed. Despite earlier references to other magistrates finding some violent offences 'understandable', one group of magistrates and one stipendiary magistrate mentioned that they found violence of any sort anathema. Finally, three magistrates who had been burgled themselves mentioned burglary (one magistrate in particular blamed the death of his mother on the burglary of her house). All such offences were those usually committed by men.

The offender at court: body language and appearance

When we're interviewing applicants to become magistrates... we say 'Have you any prejudices?'... And the stock answer is 'no'. Well that's a nonsense, isn't it? We've all got prejudices of some sort. We all have. And it's how we handle the prejudices. And so, in the days of punk, when they came into court with red hair and... earrings and all this sort of thing, then you'd find some magistrate with shock horror, you know 'Fancy coming to court dressed like that', and you would say 'Well, are you prejudiced... enough to [have] it affect your sentence?' Chairman of the Bench at one of the sample courts (M)

You know that there are certain types of people that appeal to you and certain types that don't. I have a particular problem with tattoos. I have this home-spun theory that tattoos and crime go hand in hand. I mean, I would say that 90% of the defendants that we see have a visible tattoo. I don't know what it is - it's something they put in the dye or what, but - and usually the worse the tattoos, the more I think, 'Oh, no...'. Mag. 5, Hallam court (F)

Magistrates were divided regarding the relevance of a defendant's appearance in court. On the one hand, just over a quarter of the 33 individual magistrates and 19 groups of magistrates who discussed appearance commented that appearances were deceptive and should be ignored. On the other hand, two-thirds (22 out of 33 individual magistrates, and 12 groups out of 19) claimed that a person's appearance indicated his or her attitude to the court and court procedure, so it was seen as 'human nature' for magistrates to take this into account (though they said it should not affect the eventual sentence). Similarly, body language was seen as a key tool by most magistrates, helping them to decide not only who had respect for the court, but who was telling the truth and who was remorseful. People who appeared to be nervous or tearful generally gained the sympathy of the magistrates – again, this tended to be female offenders – as long as the magistrates believed that the behaviour was genuine:

...I think it is just a feeling that they are either genuine or not - this is where the wiles of women play a part. You can be easily swayed into believing a woman is really contrite. Mag. 5, Shelley court (M)

While many said that first impressions were often misleading and should not be relied upon, three individuals and one group specifically commented on how difficult it was to make a decision without the defendant in front of them:

> *...it would be just like putting all the information into a machine*
> *and churning out the answer if... we weren't there and there wasn't*
> *a person standing in front of us.*   Mag. 6, Milton court (F)

One magistrate voiced and then disagreed with the idea that more attractive defendants seem more believable than others.   However, we note here evidence to the contrary in studies of jury decision-making (e.g. Efran 1974).   Interestingly, six female magistrates accused their male colleagues of being too quick to believe any female defendants who appeared before them – but whether this was directly related to the perceived attractiveness of defendants it was hard to tell.

Magistrates generally described themselves as being more understanding with first offenders. They recognised that people in court for the first time were likely to be nervous and unsure. If they were upset or cried, magistrates were likely to accept it as genuine. Repeat offenders, on the other hand, were viewed very differently. If they dressed up and behaved politely (addressing the magistrates and Clerk as 'Sir' or 'Ma'am'), it was seen to be a con. If they dressed down, wore a hat or put their hands in their pockets, or reacted arrogantly, they were deemed by some magistrates to have no respect for the court.   Indeed, magistrates believed that many repeat offenders deliberately defied the authority of the court by wearing hats, chewing gum, or 'playing up' to their friends at the back of the court – behaviour which prompted a negative response from the magistrates:

> *...something inside of me says 'Right, well,' you know, 'we're going*
> *to teach you a lesson, sunshine', and you tend to be more punitive.*
> Group 1, Milton court (F)

Even without a defendant's record in front of them, magistrates said they could tell the more experienced defendants from the first offenders. They gave examples of people who walked straight to the dock and let themselves in, perhaps giving their name, address and date of birth before the clerks asked for it, compared to those who had to be told where to go and when to stand and sit.

When we asked about the sentencing of women, the vast majority of the magistrates said that they rarely saw them in court (although, Criminal Statistics show that one in every six adult offenders sentenced by magistrates are female). As a result, magistrates perceived women to be less criminal, less experienced, and less likely to return to court than men. However, three individual magistrates and one group dissented from this view, arguing that for a woman to be brought to court was in itself an indication of the seriousness of her conduct.

Related to the experience of defendants and their consequent behaviour was their credibility. Magistrates were apt to believe what first offenders told them. First offenders not only generally inspired greater sympathy from magistrates, but they were inclined to attribute a first offender's body language to nervousness rather than to furtiveness or dishonesty. More experienced defendants who averted their eyes or who seemed unsure of what they were saying were assessed as likely to be lying:

> *People have mannerisms that you get the feel through... you take people not at face value, but they'll say something and you've got the feeling whether they're actually telling the truth or not - facial expressions, the way they stand.*   Group 2b, Shelley court (M)

On the other hand, as one magistrate suggested, people who argued their case too fervently were less believable than those who were more matter-of-fact in their presentation. Defendants and witnesses who used the same terminology or phrases in their testimony were thought likely to have collaborated with each other.

In line with Vennard's (1980) research of nearly 20 years ago, some Justices said they were always more inclined to believe a police officer's account than the defendant's (a third of the total number of individual magistrates, and one group mentioned this); and it was generally true that the police commanded magistrates' respect :

> *I think one tends to go with the Crown Prosecution Service and the police, if you're going to believe anybody within this set-up because [with a] police prosecution you will tend to put more weight to the police evidence than to the witnesses', especially if you are aware or have knowledge that they have a history of wrongdoing in the past.*   Mag. 9, Coleridge court (M)

Despite this, a significant number of magistrates (10 out of the 15 who discussed the point) thought that police officers were just as capable of lying as the defendants and observed that police officers sometimes contradicted each other in court.

Although magistrates rarely raised the issue themselves, virtually all (34 out of the 35 individual magistrates and the nine groups who discussed the point) agreed that signs of remorse were important. Assessing remorse, however, was difficult. Pre-sentence reports (PSRs) were sometimes helpful here, although a number of magistrates treated these reports with scepticism – a point which we touch on again later in this report. Additionally, an offender may show remorse through physical means, such as repairing damaged property of their own volition or writing a letter of apology to the victim. More frequently, however, magistrates would assess remorse themselves, based on the appearance of a defendant in court and on their own 'gut feeling':

> ... *If people can't hold their heads up, then I credit them with a sense of remorse and a sense of guilt and honesty, and if they find difficulty and [are] shifty in the eyes, I think 'you are avoiding me', but I also have to try and detect whether they feel ashamed of themselves and they can't lift their heads, and they say 'Yes, I am sorry' and their heads are down, and I have to really look at the personality as best I can, and see what they are telling me from their stance.* Mag. 4, Shelley court (M)

More cynically, magistrates often said that they wondered if people were sorry for committing an offence, or sorry that they were caught.

Generally, female defendants were perceived to be deferential and respectful. They were not only more likely to cry than men, but they were widely perceived to be less threatening in their behaviour and appearance, and so more deserving of compassion. Once again, however, there were exceptions. A male magistrate from Shelley court (Mag. 4) was keen to distinguish between 'nice ladies' and 'ladies that are far short of being ladies'. Such a stance reflects an expectation of higher morality on the part of women. The claim '*I expect women to know better*' (Mag. 1, Byron court (F)) was not uncommon in informal discussion with magistrates, though formal questioning on this point produced a rather more guarded response.

Previous researchers and those responsible for the training of magistrates within the Judicial Studies Board consider cultural background to be a strong influence on how a person uses body language, as well as its meaning and interpretation, but this was mentioned by only a quarter of individual magistrates and a third of the groups. In the context of the courtroom, cultural differences in eye contact and body posture may sway a magistrate's opinion about whether a defendant is respectful, believable, deceitful or remorseful. A small number of magistrates considered that minority ethnic group males could be perceived as arrogant in court. As the magistrates put it:

> .. *you have to be very careful because West Indians, for example, come bouncing into court - they are very loose-limbed - and you can almost interpret that as arrogance and rudeness and so on, but it is not - it is just their way of behaving... and Asians tend to be rather arrogant looking.* Mag. 5, Shelley court (M)

> *Well, insolence is insolence... and let's be honest, there's far more insolence... with ethnic minorities.*   Group 1, Shelley court (M)

> *..some of the Asians may not look you in the face, which doesn't mean to say that they are not telling the truth, because they would revere you, whereas the West Indians would look you in the face and swear that black was white...*   Mag. 14, Byron court (F)

Two individual magistrates and one group also commented that the interpretation of body language was especially difficult if a defendant or witness was using an interpreter.

Eleven of the 30 individuals and eight out of 10 groups who discussed Human Awareness training or specific training on ethnic issues had received significant input (i.e., beyond learning which name was the surname for Asian defendants or witnesses). Nineteen individual magistrates and two groups, on the other hand, claimed that they had received no training whatsoever in this area. Magistrates had mixed views as to whether any special training regarding ethnicity and cultural factors was necessary, but many believed that they could rely as much on what their family and friends told them about body language as on such training from the courts. Others (four individual magistrates and 4 groups) said they relied on 'life experience' to make them aware of cultural differences in behaviour. A number of Justices (four individuals and two groups) added that they 'bend over backwards' to be fair to ethnic minorities, specifically because the magistrates do not wish to appear biased against them.

A magistrate at Byron court, who described herself as West Indian, reported that she was very frustrated with the ignorance of her colleagues about ethnic and cultural differences. A West Indian magistrate at Milton court commented that his colleagues may not think that culture and ethnicity have a bearing on their decisions, but that they invariably do. Magistrates at Hallam court were most inclined to brush away concern about ethnic minority issues because they saw such defendants in court so rarely. Interestingly, we noted that a book in their coffee room (*Black People in the Magistrates' Courts* – produced by the Justices' Clerks' Society) warned that this was not an acceptable excuse.

Other players

Magistrates described their decisions as resulting from a complex interplay between defendants and witnesses, as well as between solicitors, court workers and the magistrates themselves. This interplay can helpfully be described by depicting the court hearing as a play, with a variety of players and elements of stagecraft:

> 'It is pure theatre, is a court. Because you get your tragedy, you get
> your melodrama, you get all facets of life...passing through it. You
> get all sorts of offences, from trivial incidents to the [very serious].
> You get your advocates, some of whom take [over] the stage, to the
> audience which is the way they are ... It is theatre. And having
> said that it's a theatre, the whole structure is based on
> communication, both visual and audible.' Mag.2, Hallam court (M)

Such an analogy is one frequently employed by researchers. Pat Carlen
(1976), for example, used the imagery of the theatre to describe the
workings of the magistrates' courts, and Paul Rock, writing about the Crown
Court, refers to the theatricality of the court and the way in which solicitors
can play up to this (1993:55-6).

Theatre performances, of course, generally involve a number of players and
each player is perceived in a different way. It follows that the weight put on
information depends on whether it comes from a Portia, an Iago or a
Polonius. A quarter of individual magistrates and groups mentioned that the
source of information affected their perception of it and that identical
information received from a defence solicitor, prosecutor, probation officer
or court clerk could weigh quite differently in their decisions.

A third of the groups of magistrates interviewed and 16 individual
magistrates expressed the belief that because defence solicitors are paid to
do the best for their clients, and are not under oath, they will say anything to
get their client off, including emphasising cultural stereotypes for female
defendants in order to gain the sympathy of the bench:

> For all the business of a man and a woman having equal rights ...,
> the solicitors bring forward the old-fashioned...'this is a woman here
> who is a family....carer, and the man's out providing', and they
> throw that forward. So that would influence the decision, because
> it's been said that these children are going to suffer if this woman
> goes away. You [won't really] get it said that the children are going
> to suffer because the man's going away. You might get the wife who
> will suffer, but it's very rarely the same argument. So a lot of the
> decisions in mitigation come from the solicitors and their attitudes.
> That makes a difference. Group 1, Hallam court (M)

However, some magistrates were more willing to distinguish between
individuals:

If the excuse is made and it comes through a reputable solicitors, then I would accept it. Now, there's the odd solicitor in those courts that I would, when he says that his client was sick, I would like to see his sick note. Mag.9, Hallam court (M)

and, on occasion, some solicitors clearly saw the need to distance themselves from their clients:

[Information] is usually prefaced by 'my instructions are', which means 'Believe this if you're stupid enough. Mag. 2, Coleridge court (F)

'I have known my client for many years'. That is an immediate give away. In other words, 'He's an absolute so-and-so and we might as well both face up to it ...', and there are a number of these gambits .... Group 5, Hallam court (F)

Overall, magistrates seemed to be rather sceptical of information from defence solicitors in general, and from certain defence solicitors in particular. In contrast, Crown Prosecution Service lawyers were often viewed as being impartial:

[Prosecutors] don't play emotional cards at all [but] rely on the absolute facts. Mag 2, Shelley court (M)

Prosecutors were rarely perceived to be representing the victim(s), but instead were seen as presenting a case on behalf of the State. As a result, magistrates were often inclined to accept the prosecutor's recommendations unless the defence could convince them otherwise:

If the prosecution asks for custody, I think that's what we should be thinking of ... We don't often disagree with their advice, do we? Group 2, Hallam court (F)

Probation officers seemed to be regarded, by at least some magistrates, with the same suspicion as defence solicitors. Roughly a quarter of the individual magistrates and seven of the groups viewed probation officers as being on the defendant's side, while only 36 of the 73 magistrates interviewed individually and only one of the 23 groups believed that probation officers presented an impartial view. In the words of one (male) magistrate at Coleridge court, some PSRs 'could have been written by Walt Disney himself'. A common reason put forward for this distrust was that probation officers' universally failed to recommend custody – those who expressed this view seemed unaware that doing so would contravene the Probation Service's National Standards (Home Office, 1995). Further, probation reports were seen by these interviewees as 'mere opinion' which were primarily based on discussions with the defendant, rather than reflecting a more objective 'professional opinion'. Psychiatric reports, on the other hand, were seen as the outcome of a professional assessment and therefore unquestionable. Although we were not able to get a clear impression of why this should be, except perhaps:

> *You have the mystique of the medical man who knows, who is qualified, and what he says goes.* Mag.10, Byron court (M)

Despite these comments, over half of all the magistrates interviewed seemed to value pre-sentence reports (and indeed, the statistics show high concordance rates between the sentencing proposals in PSRs and the actual sentences passed). When discussing PSRs and sentencing proposals for women, a number of magistrates said that they thought one reason probation officers frequently recommend probation orders for female offenders, and they followed such proposals, was because women are more likely to respond to such orders than men.

Clerks to the justices were viewed differently again:

> *We feel that they're part of our team. It's not three magistrates and a clerk, it's we're all together, and we're all part of the team.* Group 1, Hallam court (F)

The magistrates found clerks to be an invaluable resource for their decision-making, though they were quick to emphasise that the decisions were still their own. While the clerks played a lesser role when sitting with the stipendiary magistrates or with very experienced benches, we observed them leading the court procedure and doing virtually all the talking when sitting with other benches, leaving the magistrates little to say beyond announcing the sentence in some cases. Indeed, some magistrates felt that they ignored Clerks' advice 'at their peril' (7 individuals and 3 groups specifically mentioned this), perhaps because their legal training conferred the status of expert. Similarly, most lay magistrates viewed the performance of stipendiaries as setting the standard to which they should aspire and their views were considered to be influential.

The decision–makers themselves

The interplay between the magistrates themselves appeared to be at least as important to their decision-making as the advice from other 'players' in the court. Experience on the Bench, gender and personality, for instance, blended or clashed in the magistrates' efforts to reach decisions:

In your first year, you are very quiet, even though you have opinions, you feel that you just don't know enough. Mag.15, Byron court (F)

On occasion, seniority in terms of experience could even override training in the hierarchy. For example, one of the clerks at Milton court pointed out that some very experienced magistrates who have not been through the Chairmanship Training course sometimes resisted conceding the Chair - as they should - to less experienced, but trained colleagues. However, this dominance was not always actively asserted, but was sometimes the result of the deference shown to the more experienced magistrates by others:

... I have sat in courts where there have been three of us and I have had a really forceful chairman, and the other person has been as useful as a weak drink of water, and basically has .... whatever is suggested, they will go along with on the basis that Mr X has been a chairman for many years and so must know what he is doing. I don't accept that, you see. Mag. 2, Milton court (F)

As a chairperson, you can very easily influence someone, quite easily, particularly if you've got a new magistrate, you know, who might be quiet. Mag. 3, Coleridge court (M)

Some Chairmen and women seemed to be aware of their position and said that they always sought the views of the other magistrates on the bench before giving their own opinion (5 individuals and 3 groups mentioned this) but we only occasionally observed this in the context of our group discussions. More usually, we witnessed the less experienced magistrates waiting for the more experienced ones to state their opinions.

Many magistrates seemed to have the distinct impression that male and female magistrates may sentence differently:

Women are much tougher on these issues than men are ... They're much harder, much more rigid than we soft men. Group 5, Hallam court (M)

A number of magistrates said this may be more due to personalities than sex. However, seven female magistrates commented that their male colleagues were sometimes more sympathetic towards, and possibly 'taken in' by, female defendants. They believed that many male magistrates experienced discomfort in dealing with female defendants and would defer to their female colleagues:

> *Particularly being a woman, if you sit with two men, they sort of look at you as if to say, you know, 'This is your domain' and, you know 'What should we do?'... I think it's almost that they're conscious that there is a kind of 'political correctness' issue floating around in the room, and that they're careful to make sure that they get your opinion before they say anything, so they can make sure they're not about to say something that offends.* Mag. 11 Shelley court (F)

Some magistrates (7 individuals and 3 groups) had the impression that, as a result of the male magistrates' hesitance in dealing with female defendants, female magistrates' sentencing seemed more severe.

Other magistrates (4 individuals and one group) believed that *approaches* to decision-making differ between male and female magistrates as well. A female magistrate at Hallam court for example, commented that men are more 'logical' in their decisions, while women are more 'intuitive', though the decision they reach may be the same. However, such views came from men too:

> *I'm a dreadful chauvinist. I really am. But women **are** different in things like this, and I would much sooner see experienced women taking the lead in sentencing like that, and I could perhaps challenge anything that struck me as being a bit weird. But they probably have a more instinctive understanding of what's going on and what you do to put it right, which is **not** abdicating responsibility. It's trying to be realistic about the way human beings are.* Mag. 8, Coleridge court (M) (emphasis in original)

Whether any such difference was borne out in practice or had any bearing on the eventual decisions made is unclear. What is clear *is* that magistrates certainly saw gender as playing a role *between* the magistrates as they formed their decisions, as well as in relation to the defendants.

Overall, magistrates portrayed decision–making as being as much about diplomacy and negotiation as about judgement as they sought a compromise in the retiring room. The ability to compromise depended on the individual personalities on the bench, as well as on sex, ethnicity, experience, and so on – something of which most magistrates were aware:

> *In the magistracy you have all extremes, all people, some who are as someone put in this morning 'Genghis Khan' and others who are heading towards being social workers all the time.* Mag. 7, Byron court (F)

[The Bench] may be influenced by a strong-minded individual, or a forceful chair, or someone with a forceful personality, who can sort of impose his opinion – or her opinion – on others by the virtue of the argument, and I suppose the strength of their feeling. Mag. 8, Hallam court (M)

...there are only one or two, mainly gentlemen, that are really dogmatic and who won't budge. Mag. 13, Byron court (F)

The magistrates interviewed in the course of this study were very conscious of public perceptions of their sentencing practices. They felt obliged to dress and behave in court in ways which maintained the dignity of the court, which included avoiding any display of emotion in court. As a male magistrate in Shelley court explained, magistrates must 'pull the shutters down' when they come into court, and should not show any facial expression, even if something amusing or distressing happens. Some were conscious of a fear not to 'say anything stupid'. Others had bad memories of announcing a decision only to have the Clerk tell them that they could not take that course of action (a point which increases the image of the Clerk being the one in charge). Those interviewed were also concerned about the *public assessments* of their decisions (although they disagreed as to whether this would *affect* their decisions). At least some magistrates in all five courts (21 individuals and 6 groups in total) believed that the public perceived the decisions in court as 'soft'. They credited this primarily to public misunderstanding of their decisions but were nevertheless often concerned that a decision perceived as 'soft' may undermine the credibility of the court. Interestingly, such concern about self-image is borne out by the research findings of an investigation of public attitudes towards sentencing. Hough (1996) has recently revealed that members of the public are highly cynical about the ability and performance of sentencers, believing them to give sentences which are far too soft.

Magistrates said they were particularly conscious of the views of local communities in making bail decisions, but this was only one of a number of factors they would consider. They also disagreed about the extent of their accountability to the public. A number saw themselves as public servants who needed to take public opinion into account in determining the appropriate response to certain types of crime and the severity of their sentences (11 individuals and 5 groups, that is, 69% of those who specifically addressed the issue, or 15% of all magistrates). Others removed themselves from 'the public' to some extent, suggesting that, people will not understand sentencing until they sit in the court themselves and try to deal with specific cases:

...they're all hangers and floggers, out in the community. Within the community, they don't realise that there's a vast machinery working to try and rehabilitate offenders. Chairman of the Bench at one of the sample courts (M)

Some magistrates also felt that the options open to them were restricted by organisational or managerial factors beyond their control:

You can't fine a lot ... We can go with our Guidelines, we can go with what we feel, and we can go with seriousness of the offence, but when it comes down to the nitty gritty, it's ability to pay and the time that the court's got to collect it. Mag. 1, Hallam court (F)

Although the majority believed that The Magistrates' Sentencing Guidelines allowed them ample freedom to impose the sentences they believed were appropriate (with the notable exception of the penalties available in the Youth Court), managerial concerns were thought to be influencing decisions in the court. (Twenty-four out of the 38 individual magistrates and 10 out of the 16 groups who discussed this expressed such a view.) Fines are the most obvious example of this. Magistrates explained that the Lord Chancellor's Department has been putting pressure on the courts to have fines paid within a specified period of time, and that the Justices' Clerks in each court were enforcing this. As a result, magistrates were feeling forced to impose lower financial penalties than they thought appropriate in order to increase the chances of payment within the set period. The financial cost of certain disposals was also occasionally a factor in magistrates' decisions, most notably in balancing the cost of custody for female defendants with the cost (financial or otherwise) of putting children into care. However, magistrates expressed less concern about the space available in prisons for remand or sentence. One individual and one group even commented:

That wouldn't influence me if I had someone on a very serious offence. As far as I was concerned, I would remand him in custody, and it's up to the Home Secretary to find him a place. That's not my job; my job is to consider the facts. Mag. 3, Coleridge court (M)

Finally, some magistrates (3 individuals and 2 groups) expressed concern about the limited availability of certain options, particularly in relation to female offenders. For example, a few magistrates said that they hesitated to impose Community Service Orders on women because there may not be suitable work available for them. Similarly, some magistrates had experienced difficulty in the past with probation programmes for women which were delayed until enough women had been sentenced to such a programme for it to proceed (e.g., all-female counselling groups). Finally, three magistrates commented that they hesitated to impose custody on women because the women's prisons were too far away for the women to be able to maintain family ties. None of these difficulties were raised as being relevant to male offenders.

Dealing with the troubled and troublesome: help or punishment?

The magistrates' impressions of defendants as 'troubled' or 'troublesome', whether based on the offence itself or on other factors, appeared to influence the outcome of both bail and sentencing decisions. 'Troubled' offenders were seen by magistrates to need help more than punishment, whereas 'troublesome' offenders were seen to deserve punishment both for their own sake, and to deter others.

'Help' was interpreted in many different forms. Probation was seen to be the most common source of 'help' for offenders, despite the fact that almost all the magistrates acknowledged that probation orders are intended to encompass other sentencing objectives, including punishment. Magistrates often classified female offenders as being in need of help: with running the household, with organising finances, and (in 'Jane's' case) with controlling their emotions:

> *...probation is the best thing, because they're not really naughty, they just need help and support...Whereas perhaps with men, people see it more as a straight financial choice, and so hurting them financially with a fine is what's required.* Mag. 11, Shelley court (F)

In contrast, men were only seen as needing help when they had the responsibility of raising children on their own (which virtually never happened). Men who were unemployed, for example, were seen as 'layabouts', whereas women who were unemployed were 'doing all they could' to take care of their children.

Other types of punishments could also be seen as 'doing the offender a favour' both because they were noncustodial and because of their intrinsic characteristics. Community Service Orders (CSOs) were one of these, where offenders were seen as being encouraged to do something constructive with their lives. Three individual magistrates commented that a CSO could lead to job opportunities in the future. However, as Barker (1993) also found, Community Service Orders were seen as an option for women only if there were care facilities for the children and if the woman could do something suitable (again, usually a care role). A number of magistrates (4 individual magistrates and 2 groups) commented that they almost never sentenced a female offender to a CSO.

Magistrates perceived their use of custody for women as a sentence of last resort, employed either because the crime was so serious that prison was the only option, or because they felt forced into it by the legislation, such as for non-payment of fines. In contrast, men were open to any sort of penalty, though tended to be given probation orders if their offence involved the use of drugs or alcohol, or involved motor vehicles. Male offenders reached the custody threshold much faster than women, either because of the motivation for the offence (e.g. it was inspired by 'greed' rather than 'need'), or because they had relatively limited mitigation compared to women (e.g. no direct responsibility for child care, at least in the view of the magistrates). We should acknowledge, however, that magistrates declared that custody was a rare option for both men and women.

Only a few magistrates (4 individuals and one group) believed that prison could help either male or female offenders in addition to punishing them, either through training or education, or by restricting access to drugs, alcohol, or people who were bad influences on their behaviour. Similarly, 'protection' was one of the grounds for remanding someone in custody. This could be protection from others who would try to avenge a crime or, in some cases, to help *prevent* someone from committing suicide. Prevention of suicide is included on Bail Forms as an exception to the Bail Act 1976 – in other words, as a justification for denying bail.

Conclusion

What emerges from the interviews with magistrates is a complexity that goes well beyond a simple male/female offender distinction, but appears to be closely tied to it. Magistrates generally seemed to make distinctions between offenders depending on whether they could understand the offence as a matter of survival, see it as a result of provocation or coercion, or attribute it to illness rather than irresponsibility.

How magistrates perceived defendants in the courtroom is influenced by considerations other than the simple 'facts of the case'. Appearance and demeanour, the novice status of first-timers or 'know it all' status of experienced offenders, the 'believability' of defendants, expressions and perceptions of remorse, and the reading or misreading of cues about ethnicity and culture all seemed to play a part in shaping magistrates' perceptions of the offenders before them. Such factors cut across simple sex differences, but we can surmise that the relative inexperience of female defendants and their concomitant 'nervousness' might lead magistrates to view them as more 'believable' than others – a point which reiterates the findings of Hedderman (1990) in earlier research. Additionally, women's relative inexperience in offending might be reflected in their behaviour in court - showing deference and remorse – thus leading the magistrates to view them more sympathetically than some of the male defendants who were experienced offenders, well-rehearsed in courtroom procedures and thus seemingly less remorseful.

A distinction between 'troubled' and 'troublesome' offenders was, thus based on the perceived motivation for the offence and the demeanour of defendants in court. In turn, magistrates may make different decisions for bail and certainly choose different options for sentencing. They appeared to favour the use of probation orders or discharges for women – the 'troubled' offenders - as a means of assisting rather than just punishing them. Only occasionally did magistrates believe that male offenders merited assistance, and sometimes 'assistance' for men came in the form of CSOs or custody. Even allowing for the fact that women were more likely to be first offenders or less frequent offenders than men, and were more likely to behave respectfully in court, on the basis of these interviews it would seem that magistrates are less inclined to sympathise with men and to impose a sentence intended to address their underlying problems and needs. This pattern becomes clearer in the next Chapter when we consider more fully the personal and family circumstances which magistrates take into consideration when sentencing men and women.

4 Forms of mitigation

Magistrates were unanimous in arguing that, while the nature of the offence, motivation, and behaviour in court all set the parameters for their decision-making, the offender's personal circumstances could also play a part.

What type of circumstances did magistrates believe were relevant to their decisions? To what extent did their expectations of what was 'normal' shape this? We asked magistrates about a range of factors including family responsibilities, family history, employment and area of residence to see what made them more or less sympathetic to offenders (what would mitigate or aggravate) and how this affected their decisions.

Family responsibilities

While defence solicitors frequently mentioned children or partners (particularly pregnant partners) in mitigation for male and female clients, magistrates gave little credence to such arguments when dealing with the majority of male defendants. Magistrates were clear that being a parent would only mitigate against a sentence for a man if he was a single parent with sole responsibility for his children.

In contrast, over 80 per cent of the magistrates who took part in individual or group interviews said that female offenders invariably had childcare responsibilities, and that they believed that women with children should be kept out of prison. The magistrates explained that, in their experience, women who came to court tended to be single mothers. Imprisoning such women might well lead to their children going into care, penalising the family rather than the offender alone and adding childcare costs to that of providing custody. Indeed, 10 individuals and three groups of magistrates said that women with children should be kept out of custody, regardless of whether another carer was available, because children need their mothers. After mild prompting, in which the interviewer described a range of different forms of support women might have available (e.g., sister, mother, or male partner) to see where magistrates would draw the line, seven individuals and two groups said that the availability of another carer would reduce the relevance of children as a mitigation. Where the only other potential carer was a woman's male partner, however, two of these magistrates specifically commented that they would not assume that such a relationship was stable enough to entrust the man with responsibility for childcare. In this sense, therefore, mitigation because of children was on a graduated scale, with single mothers or 'unstable' partnerships having most impact on magistrates' decision-making, where magistrates were concerned that children might end up in care. It is important to note, however, that at least some of the 61 per cent of women in prison whom a recent study showed to be primary child-carers (Caddle and Crisp, 1997) were probably sent there by magistrates – suggesting that what magistrates do, and what they think they do, may differ.

Magistrates also said that they tended to rule out Community Service Orders for most women because of their childcare responsibilities.[1] Similarly, magistrates said that fining a woman could have implications for her children, but saw fining a man as only having consequences for him. Having dependent children did not give women a licence to commit crime, but their existence could supersede the influence of factors such as offence seriousness on the sentence for women, even though at least some magistrates recognised that they were responding to 'children' as a cultural stereotype rather than to an individual woman's childcare responsibilities:

> *I've often asked myself the question, to what extent we reinforce stereotypes in the courts, because women **are** seen to be the primary carers. They're not... in all cases...the primary carers. Sometimes if they – they're working, for example, and the husband is the house-husband... and **he's** the primary carer... sometimes... we don't really maintain objectivity as much as... perhaps we should.* Group 1, Milton court (F) (emphasis in original)

Interestingly, when asked specifically about the sentencing of childless women, a number of magistrates (9 individual magistrates, all men) commented that women should be kept out of custody in general – that they should treat 'the fairer sex as the fairer sex' (Mag. 4, Hallam court) - even if they had no children. They believed there was something 'wrong' about remanding or sentencing a woman to custody, so they would be more hesitant to resort to custody than they would in an equivalent case involving a man.

The differential treatment of men and women was not, therefore, *solely* due to having responsibility for children, but the powerfulness of this responsibility as a mitigating factor was unmistakable. Magistrates had mixed

---

1 Magistrates interviewed in this study seemed largely unaware that many probation services will pay for childcare to ensure that women are not automatically debarred from CS. One reason for this may be that PSR writers themselves do not know about such arrangements (HMI Probation, 1996).

reactions to the question of whether dependants such as elderly parents would mitigate in the same way as children would. Their initial response was usually that this almost never came up, but then they added that if it did, they would take it into consideration. While most said that other dependants would mitigate to a similar extent (a view held by 20 out of the 29 and 6 out of the 8 groups of magistrates who discussed it), the remainder were of the opinion that this would be less influential:

> ...*the poor, ageing, ailing [parents] are usually dragged out of the cupboard for convenience.* Mag. 11, Hallam court (F)

Some explained that such mitigation would depend on the extent of the disability, but others commented that elderly people were more likely to have other people available to care for them. Other magistrates believed that children were a more important consideration because they were more malleable and vulnerable. They concluded that the elderly, on the other hand, had lived their lives and were not likely to be damaged in the long term from the loss of the defendant's care.

Family structure and social control

> *I think that's evident, in quite a lot of cases, that usually criminality starts from a break-up in the family structure.*
> Chairman of one of the sample courts (M)

An offender's family structure seemed to be of interest to magistrates in a variety of contexts. Children were a chief mitigating factor, as mentioned above. Although they did not mitigate to the same extent, parents and other family members also added to the 'jigsaw' – as magistrates described the process of decision-making – because it influenced their impression of whether the offender's environment placed him or her at risk of further offending. For example, three magistrates commented that in dealing with young offenders from single parent families they were conscious that this background failed to provide the atmosphere of discipline necessary to prevent further offending.

Family structure seemed to feature particularly prominently when we asked about the decision to grant bail. First, extended families seemed to pose particular problems when setting conditions of residence. For example, on more than one occasion we observed cases of defendants who resided at one address during the week, then at another address (e.g. with a grandparent) at the weekend – a situation which often flummoxed the magistrates. Second, magistrates were clearly confused when they learned that someone described as the defendant's 'uncle' was not a blood relation.

Third, from their comments, we judged that magistrates took being married as a sign of stability whereas cohabiting was regarded as a more transient state:

> *Marriage means stability. It means commitment. And otherwise, what's to stop anybody [from] going together a few months and then disappearing, which is what they do.* Mag. 3, Shelley court (M)

> *One of our last stipendiaries said to me that the courts would be more useful if they were a marriage bureau or some sort... because people will either stop offending because they've married and got a 'good woman' quite probably, or because they've died!*   G r o u p 3, Shelley court (F)

However, living with someone else was always a better state to be in than living alone, because it provided a degree of 'social control'. Single people, particularly young people, who lived on their own were viewed as being more of a risk than others because of the perceived lack of supervision or stability in their lives:

> *If they're girls, they invite the lads in to knock them [up].... If they're lads, they're into drugs because there's nobody to keep an eye on them.* Stipe. at one of the sample courts (M)

From the interviews it became clear that magistrates tended to believe that men should live either with parents or preferably with a wife or girlfriend. Women too should live with their parents or husbands (or long-term partner), or at least have family in the area, though responsibility for children was in itself also recognised as exerting a controlling influence. In this sense, partners or family perhaps provided support for a woman with children, but social control and stability for a man.

Ten of the 19 individual magistrates who discussed it, baulked at the idea of a homosexual partnership being able to provide the same stability as a heterosexual one. (In fact, only a few of the justices had come across this situation in practice.)

Magistrates gave credit to defendants who had partners or relatives (especially parents or grandparents in the case of young offenders) with them at court, which they saw as evidence of the family's concern and support for the defendant. Further, magistrates gleaned extra information from the demeanour and body language of the family and friends who came to court. People who did not have parents or partners in the gallery gave magistrates the impression that they had little social support and might therefore be a bail risk. Support from peers, however, could actually act against the defendant. A few magistrates believed that defendants who had a 'fan club' in the gallery would play up to this and behave arrogantly to impress their friends (5 individuals and 2 groups of magistrates mentioned this). This type of 'support' could even adversely affect the bail decision. Interestingly, two magistrates commented that people from ethnic minorities (Asian males in particular) were more likely than others to have a 'fan club' present in court.

There was general agreement that *current* family circumstances were more likely to mitigate than an offender's *background*. For example, being the head of a one-parent family was more influential than coming from a one-parent family, and being abused was more important than having been abused as a child. However, opinions were divided on whether background had any substantive effect:

> *...the fact that their father abused them as a child if they are adults, it is an adult world – the world doesn't owe them anything; they have got to stand on their own two feet and accept responsibility for their actions. We all have to do it.*   Mag. 8, Byron court (M)

> *Personally I would be more inclined to punish heavier someone who'd had every chance, coming from a home background than someone who clearly had been brought up in deprived conditions.*
> Group 3, Byron court (M)

This division was most apparent during the magistrates' discussions of the 'Jane' case study. While some magistrates believed that information about her childhood was irrelevant, others argued that this information would mitigate, as it explained her present concerns and reaction to them.

Magistrates seemed to make little distinction between male and female offenders in terms of family history.

Employment and income

The four courts we visited were all in areas of relatively high unemployment, which meant not only that most defendants in court were unemployed – as most magistrates recognised – but also that magistrates wanted to make sure that those who had jobs could keep them. Two Justices were blunt enough to say that unemployed defendants were 'layabouts' who leeched off the state to supplement their life of crime. They excepted women caring full-time for small children from this, considering them to have no time for anything else (even Community Service).

Being employed was viewed very positively for a number of reasons. First, it was seen as ensuring that people were occupied (and thus had less time to commit offences than they would if they were unemployed). Second, magistrates also tended to see employed offenders as hard-working, as doing something constructive for themselves, supporting their families, and putting something back into the community (unless, of course, the person had offended against an employer).

Magistrates regarded people who came to court with the *promise* of employment with scepticism. Some even joked that coming to court was one of the fastest cures for unemployment. However, even a job prospect could mitigate if a defendant brought the court proof of a job offer.

It was clear from magistrates' comments that the use of fines and compensation was directly linked to income, and thus (indirectly) to employment:

> ... *at the back of my mind often, I feel: are we guilty of punishing people for being poor?*   Group 3, Byron court (M)

If the offender had no (declared) income beyond State benefits, magistrates described themselves as facing a frustrating choice between resorting to other options or imposing what they saw as a 'derisory' fine. If they sentenced someone to a CSO or to custody because he or she had no money to pay a fine, they felt that they were discriminating against people who had no money. On the other hand, fining an unemployed offender £50 where an employed person would have been fined a much larger sum seemed to disproportionately penalise an offender for having an income.

Six individual magistrates and three groups commented that an offender's income or family responsibilities should not justify altering the nature of a penalty from a fine to another order, but only the size of the fine (the legally correct decision). However, most magistrates seemed to think that moving between types of penalties was a practical necessity.

For unemployed male offenders at least, magistrates said they would often resort to a nominal fine, based on the offender's means, in place of the higher amount they otherwise considered appropriate to the offence. However, when we asked why men might be given fines while women were discharged or put on probation (see Part I), a third of the individuals and the groups responded that this was because such women had no money of their own (and because they were usually responsible for dependent children).

The question of dependence on another person's income raises an important issue: to what extent should a financial penalty be based on a 'household' income rather than on the income of the offender? Twenty-four of the 30 individuals and six of the seven groups who discussed this point believed that penalties should be assessed on the basis of the household income, if that income is given in court. Most said that they based this on the assumption that, traditionally, the woman was the care-taker while the man was the wage-earner. The woman was therefore entitled to a housekeeping allowance, and was also the one to claim any Family Benefit.

Such a view assumes that a reciprocal relationship exists in the household. However, this may be unrealistic, for example, where the woman is a victim of domestic violence (see, for example, Yllö 1993). As one magistrate explained to another in one of our group discussions:

> *Well, maybe in your house there **is** one pot of money, but I suspect in some households there are **two** separate pots of money, and her pot happens to be empty. And if... she is told to pay compensation and has no money, and her husband says, 'Well, I'm sorry, but you're not having any of mine, dear,' where is she?* Group 1, Shelley court (M) (emphasis in original)

This also begs the question of whether it is appropriate to penalise the non-offending wage earner for the offences committed by his or her partner. It is perhaps helpful to draw an analogy with the Youth Court, where parents are held financially responsible for their children's behaviour; we might question whether partners should be deemed responsible for each other's behaviour in the same way, and indeed, whether the idea of a 'household income' works the same way for a man as for a woman – a point which remains for further research.

The magistrates mainly considered awarding compensation for violent offences or in cases where the cost of property damage or theft could be assessed with a reasonable degree of accuracy. For violent offences, awarding compensation was heavily influenced by the role of the victim in the offence. The decision to award compensation also took the offender's income into account, although this did not stop magistrates from imposing compensation in either case study where 'Jason' was receiving benefits, and 'Jane' was dependent on her husband's income.

We also asked magistrates if voluntary work could mitigate in the same way as paid employment. Only two interviewees claimed to have dealt with offenders in this position. Of the small number of magistrates (7) who compared them, five did not put the same weight on voluntary work as on paid employment because voluntary work could be continued relatively easily following a CSO or time in custody, whereas paid employment might be lost altogether. Further, loss of voluntary work was thought to have less of an impact on a family than would a loss of income. The other two argued that voluntary work could mitigate, as it reflected positively on the character of the defendant. The magistrates made no distinction between male and female defendants in this respect.

Conclusion

The results of our discussions with magistrates about what sorts of factors might mitigate sentencing decisions for men and women suggest that female defendants were likely to find mitigation in dependants, primarily children, whereas men rarely benefitted from the fact of having dependent children.

Most magistrates had fairly firm views regarding the type of social structure which provided enough stability and discipline to influence a bail or sentencing decision in a positive way. The support of family or long-term partners, preferably in the same house, materially improved both male and female defendants' chances of avoiding custody and possibly mitigated against the eventual sentence as well. Family history too may have a bearing, but would depend more on its interaction with other features of the case.

Paid employment often mitigated in remand and sentencing decisions for those defendants fortunate enough to have it, but the lack of full-time employment seemed to be viewed less negatively for women than men because magistrates believed that most of the women they dealt with were mothers who were (and should be) occupied with childcare. On the other hand, paid employment often resulted in larger financial penalties for men. As Part I of the current study shows, however, this does not always result in women being dealt with more leniently.

The locality and permanence of a defendant's address was acknowledged to play some part in bail decisions, but not on sentencing. Magistrates did not generally distinguish between male and female defendants in their comments about these factors.

While all of these factors – family circumstances and background, employment, and locality – may have a bearing on the decisions magistrates make, they will not necessarily in themselves have a material impact on a decision. For this reason, we asked magistrates whether each particular factor would push a potential penalty up or down if the case were on the borderline. Interestingly, and consistent with the results from Part I, the borderlines seemed to differ greatly for men and women. The custody threshold showed the clearest difference here, with magistrates doing everything possible to keep a woman out of custody, but sentencing men primarily in response to the seriousness of their offending. They also avoided using fines for women, but used them frequently for men. Much of this seemed to be based on the fact that magistrates considered family circumstances and responsibilities to be much more relevant when dealing with female than with male offenders. Therefore, although personal circumstances carried weight for both groups, they were given more weight with regard to female offenders.

The patterns of mitigation, particularly as they relate to men and women, clearly reflect the same divisions between 'troubled' offenders (those who deserve sympathy and assistance) and 'troublesome' offenders (those who deserve punishment). The issues are exceedingly complex, however, and reflect considerations of family responsibilities, family structure and the potential for social control through the family, the influence of family history as mitigation, employment and income and the links between these factors and the ability to pay fines and compensation. Some of these factors, but by no means all, appeared to carry differential degrees of influence depending on whether the magistrates were discussing men or women. Overall, magistrates appeared to consider family circumstances and responsibilities to be much more relevant in mitigation when dealing with female than with male defendants. This finding confirms the earlier research findings of Farrington and Morris (1983) and Eaton (1983, 1986) who describe family circumstances as a key factor in decision-making relating to women, but much less important in decision-making in relation to men.

5 Conclusion: Towards an understanding of the sentencing of women

The topic of sex discrimination is one on which people often hold such strong (and usually fixed) opinions. Up to this point, therefore, we have endeavoured to present the findings of this research quite straightforwardly and with only minimal interpretation. This conclusion, however, reflects the four authors' shared interpretations of both the statistical exercises described in Part I and the interviews carried out in Part II. We summarise what the research findings mean and how they feed into our understanding of the sentencing of women.

Few people would seriously contest the notion that the criminal justice system should dispense justice fairly, regardless of sex, race, class or any other improper influence. No one is more aware of this need than the magistracy, who already spend a proportion of their training on such (human awareness) issues. But what exactly does fairness consist of in this context? In our view, it lies in consistency of approach rather than uniformity of outcome. In other words, it involves asking the same questions about factors such as employment status, family responsibilities and financial circumstances regardless of the offender's sex, rather than presuming that certain questions will only apply to males or females. From this perspective, to criticise sentencing practices on the grounds that the official statistics show different sentencing patterns would be unfair and, in any case, a futile exercise. These patterns may simply reflect the fact that the men and women who come to court differ across a wide range of factors which sentencers take into consideration when determining an appropriate sentence. In order to look at whether there is disparity in sentencing decisions, one needs therefore to look at the characteristics of those coming to court and at how sentencers say they weigh these and other factors in their decision-making. This research set out to do both these things.

In our view, neither the statistical analysis described by Dowds and Hedderman nor the interviews Gelsthorpe and Loucks carried out support the contention that differences in the way men and women are sentenced by magistrates is a consequence of anything as simple as deliberate discrimination. If that were true one would expect the statistical exercise to show women consistently receiving different sentences to men. But they do not. For example, they stood an equal chance of going to prison for a first violent offence, whereas among repeat offenders, women were less likely to go to prison. And among drug offenders, women recidivists were as likely as men to be imprisoned, but first timers were not.

In fact both parts of this study suggest that sentencing decisions are the outcome of the interactive effect of a number of factors. The most important of these is the nature of the offence. However, the offender's circumstances, the way other participants in the courtroom portray the offence and offender, the offender's appearance and behaviour in court, and how the members of each bench interact are also influential. Together these factors shape the court's perception of an offender as essentially troubled or troublesome, and this in turn determines whether help or punishment is at the heart of the court's response.

Women were more likely to be defined as troubled than men. From interviews with magistrates there seem to be a number of reasons for this. First, five out of every six of the offenders magistrates routinely deal with are male and most are under 30 years of age. Perhaps because of their sheer numbers, young men are likely to be seen as troublesome and are only very rarely viewed as troubled. As we know from the statistics, the majority of the women offenders magistrates try and sentence are charged with shoplifting. Again, from the interviews with magistrates in Part II of this study, we know that magistrates generally believe that such women steal through need rather than greed, they often have sole care of young children, and they are usually living on benefits or are dependent on a partner's income. So how are these perceptions of women translated into sentencing? The most striking consequence is that, as the analyses presented in Part I show, magistrates are reluctant to fine women. Even if this difference was found to be inspired by a desire not to financially penalise a woman's family, it carries the risk that, skipping a step on the sentencing ladder this time round, will lead to an even more severe sentence being imposed in the event of a subsequent conviction. To use probation where a fine would have been appropriate is also an ineffective use of resources (Moxon et al., 1990).

Both parts of the study show that magistrates appear to favour probation or discharges for women. The interviews carried out in Part II suggest that these measures are used with the intention of assisting rather than punishing women. Unless sending women to prison was unavoidable because of the seriousness of their offending, it was usually ruled out on the grounds that it would adversely affect their children.

We know from previous research that female offenders do indeed describe themselves as stealing through need and having responsibility for dependent children (see, for example, Carlen 1988 and Morris et al., 1995). However, neither those studies nor the current research show whether they differ from men in either respect. Examination of court records to see if male and female offenders are matched in these ways has proved difficult because records do not hold such information consistently. This is certainly an issue worth examining in future research, however, as the magistrates interviewed in Part II of this study revealed that, when considering mitigation, they were not simply responding to the fact that women and men appeared in different circumstances. Thus, for example, having family responsibilities was less central to decisions about male offenders, and being employed carried less weight when the offender was a woman. Even when a man is considered to be more troubled than troublesome, this does not necessarily have the same consequences as for a woman. On the occasions when magistrates believed that male offenders merited assistance, this tended to take the form of employment training through Community Service Orders or help with alcohol or drug addiction. These findings are strikingly similar to those reported by Farrington and Morris (1983) and Mary Eaton (1983,1986). A key difference is that they reflect sentencing in the mid-1990s rather than the mid-1980s and occur in a period when a great deal of attention has been given to notions of fairness and justice and to race and gender issues in the delivery of justice.

Turning to the offender in the courtroom, while some magistrates recognised that body language is open to misinterpretation, most stressed the importance of seeing the offender in court, and a number were confident that they would not themselves misinterpret nonverbal cues. The research also indicated that, based on perceptions of body language and appearance, men – ethnic minority men in particular – may come across as having less respect for the court, while women are generally perceived to be inexperienced, deferential and (therefore) honest.

The internal politics of the courtroom also seem to shape magistrates' decision-making. The same information could be viewed quite differently according to which courtroom player provided it – most weight was accorded to information from prosecutors or the Clerk, who were regarded by magistrates as being impartial. Not only defence solicitors but probation officers were seen as siding with the offender.

Interaction between magistrates was also important, with experience weighing more heavily than training. Moreover, virtually all the magistrates mentioned 'common sense' or 'gut feelings' at some stage of their assessment as to who was respectful or rebellious, remorseful or rancorous; and 'common sense' was what magistrates used to explain any decision that seemed to have no other explanation or, at least, no easily expressed explanation. Yet notions of what is 'common sense' and what are reliable indicators of honesty and remorse differed among magistrates.

Taken as a whole, these findings suggest that there remains a risk that some magistrates will resort to their 'common sense' (and a gendered 'common-sense' at that) as the best arbiter of what is right, despite the fact that new magistrates receive training designed to inform them of the inherent dangers of making decisions on the basis of stereotypes and on the dangers of relying on non-verbal cues.

The difficulty to be addressed is one of finding ways to challenge stereotypical pictures of men and women, without ignoring the fact that they often (but *not* always) do have different needs and responsibilities (and these are often precisely the needs and responsibilities which fuel the stereotypes). It may also be that the time to recognise such differences is in the shape and content of particular sentences rather than in the choice between different levels of sentence, but discussion of this is beyond our remit. A number of changes may be helpful here:

- Increased emphasis on gender issues in training to counteract the fact that so many magistrates have comparatively little experience of dealing with women in the courtroom. This is probably best accomplished through the 'human awareness' element of magistrates' training which encourages them to reflect on how cultural and gender specific stereotypes inform their practices and perceptions in the courtroom in ways which could lead to unfair sentencing. Currently, such training tends to focus on race issues and it would be unfortunate if combining race and gender in this way masked the importance of either issue. It is also important to note that while 'human awareness training is popular, it does not appear to have been subject to any large scale or systematic evaluation.

- Training on gender (and race) should be made available to *all* magistrates rather than to new magistrates alone so as to ensure that resistant or reluctant magistrates are exposed to the issues as a matter of routine.

- Where magistrates may feel that their sentencing options are constrained by a (male or female) offender's childcare responsibilities, the Probation Service should use PSRs to draw attention to the fact that suitable childcare arrangements can be made.

- Increased feedback on sentencing patterns in each court – particularly patterns relating to men and women – may also assist magistrates in the general task of achieving consistency in approach.

Finally, we would suggest that there are at least three questions which require further exploration and discussion:

- to what extent does training help to address the tendency to use gender-stereotyping in sentencing?

- to what extent do gender, race and other factors have an interactive effect on sentencing?

- are the decisions of professional sentencers subject to the same influences as those of lay magistrates?

Appendix A: Explanation of multivarite analyses

In the present study the decision to impose a custodial sentence was examined first for each offence type (shoplifting, violent and drug offences). Bivariate analyses were carried out to identify those factors significantly related to custody and then the independent effects of each were assessed using a linear regression model. Those variables that were found to be significantly related to sentencing outcome when all the other variables were taken into account were then entered into a logistic regression analysis and a model built using a forward selection technique. The arguments for and against using a least-squares multiple regression analysis with a dichotomous dependent variable and independent variables in two or three categories, which may or may not be normally distributed, are well documented elsewhere (see for example, Farrington and Morris 1983). Statistically this method is clearly less correct but often used (at least for data reduction purposes) in place of the more statistically correct alternatives. Neither logistic regressions nor crude log-linear analyses are practically feasible when analysing large numbers of variables.

The bivariate analyses were then repeated with a dependent variable from the other end of the sentencing spectrum; that is, discharge/more severe sentence. In general the results here did not warrant further analysis as they were much weaker than those predicting custody. Throughout all these analyses those offenders on their first court appearance (hereafter called 'first offenders') were examined separately from those facing a second or subsequent appearance ('recidivists').

Following the analysis of the dichotomous dependent variables (custody/not custody, discharge/not discharge), some intermediate sentences were added into the equation. Discriminant analysis was carried out first for the three category outcomes 'discharge', 'fine', 'other more severe'; and then for the outcomes 'discharge/fine', 'other more severe non-custodial', 'prison'. Discriminant analysis is probably the most statistically correct technique to use in these circumstances (though in reality it is very similar to least-squares multiple regression). However it is usually recommended that any discriminant analysis should first be carried out on only half the sample and the resulting model then checked on the other half. This is not generally a requirement for linear regression because the 'adjusted r squared' statistic is an attempt to allow for the fact that the equation will never fit the second set of data quite as well as it did the first (from which it was constructed). However a pragmatic decision was taken not to follow this procedure here because it would result in such small numbers of women in the working samples.

Independent variables and co-linearity

One final issue is the nature of the independent variables yielded by the Offender's Index. In principle there are a great many useful pieces of information contained in this, but in practice many courts do not submit full information (ethnic group and 'plea' are often missing, TICs are not now recorded) and for analysis purposes many variables are very highly inter-correlated. For example, the fact that an offender has had at least one probation order in the past is often highly correlated with the number of previous convictions against him/her. Theoretically the two are measuring different things (sentencing history and criminal history) but in some cases variables had to be excluded from models because of co-linearity or because two variables involved almost exactly the same offenders (those who had a history of robbery and violence also tended to have a history of theft and burglary etc.). The process of removing variables before any regression analysis is necessarily somewhat subjective but variables were always excluded where one was very highly correlated with another which itself provided a stronger relationship with the sentencing outcome. The rule of thumb often used is that 'no predictor should be included that is more closely related to the best predictor than it is to the dependent variable' (Hair et al., 1987). Even when this was not the case, some variables were occasionally excluded because they were very highly correlated (.6 or higher) with other independent variables which were not necessarily highly correlated with the best predictor variable.

Where two variables were clearly co-linear (such as the number of previous appearances and the number of previous convictions) the one which was more strongly related to the sentencing outcome was kept in the equation (almost invariably previous convictions). Variables which were quite highly correlated with others but where both appeared to measure quite different theoretical constructs were kept in the analysis (e.g., the time since the last court appearance and the number of previous convictions).

Appendix B: Final logistic regression models

Table I Logistic regression modelling use of custody for shoplifters with previous convictions

Outcomes correctly classified   89.57%
-2 Log likelihood   1,521.558
Goodness of fit   2,618.572
n   2,809

	Chi-Square	df	Significance
Model Chi–Square	598.539	8	.0000

Variable	B	S.E.	Wald	df	Sig	R	Exp B
Number of current offences	.37	.030	151.93	1	.00	.27	1.44
Crown court	1.61	.161	100.88	1	.00	.22	5.03
Number of previous offences	.02	.003	45.39	1	.00	.14	1.02
Male	1.05	.223	22.19	1	.00	.10	2.85
Over 25	.61	.162	13.95	1	.00	.08	1.83
Previous suspended sentence	.58	.163	12.42	1	.00	.07	1.78
Previous youth custody	-.57	.161	12.37	1	.00	-.07	.56
Also appearing for a breach	.78	.240	10.56	1	.00	.06	2.18
Constant	-4.98	.253	387.20	1	.00	–	≠

Table 2 Logistic regression modelling use of custody for violent offenders with previous convictions

Outcomes correctly classified   84.27%
-2 Log likelihood   3,254.329
Goodness of fit   4,469.326
N   4,610

	Chi-Square	df	Significance
Model Chi–Square	1884.87	10	.0000

Variable	B	S.E.	Wald	df	Sig	R	Exp B
Crown court	2.34	.099	598.68	1	.00	.34	10.43
Number current offences	.30	.025	144.42	1	.00	.17	1.35
Serious offence	.98	.107	83.92	1	.00	.13	2.66
Male	1.61	.315	26.39	1	.00	.07	5.04
Previous custody or YC	.52	.111	21.71	1	.00	.06	1.67
Appearing for a breach	.66	.158	17.31	1	.00	.06	1.93
Prev robbery	.50	.138	12.88	1	.00	.05	1.64
Number of prev offences	.02	.005	17.33	1	.00	-.04	.96
Time since last appearance	-.04	.014	9.24	1	.00	-.04	.96
Age	-.02	.007	6.59	1	.01	-.03	.98
Constant	-4.76	.383	154.65	–	–	–	–

Table 3 Logistic regression modelling use of custody for first-time drug offenders

Outcomes correctly classified	91.87%
-2 Log likelihood	418.266
Goodness of fit	1,334.708
N	996

	Chi-Square	df	Significance
Model Chi-Square	519.90	15	.0000

Variable	B	S.E.	Wald	df	Sig	R	Exp B
Crown court	3.40	.309	120.97	1	.00	.36	29.28
Serious offence	2.54	.271	88.11	1	.00	.30	12.67
Fraud, burglary violence also	1.83	.476	14.80	1	.00	.12	6.25
Age	.054	.015	13.83	1	.00	.11	1.06
Male	1.61	.315	26.39	1	.00	.07	5.04
Constant	-7.06	.645	119.87	–	–	–	–

Appendix C: Case Studies

Pre-Sentence Report on Jane Smith

Age:　　　30　　　　　　　D.O.B:　　　17.1.65

Address:　　2 Knot Lane,

　　　　　　Davidstown,

　　　　　　Borcetshire,　B44　0TX

Offences:　Unlawful Wounding (s. 20)

For the purposes of this report I have interviewed the defendant on one occasion at the Ambridge Probation Office and on one occasion in her home.

1. *Offence*

Jane Smith has pleaded guilty to unlawful wounding. This offence is the result of a conflict between Jane Smith and Mary Ellen McDonald over relationships with Mr Smith, Jane Smith's husband. Jane Smith admits that she was extremely angry to learn that Ms McDonald had been having an affair with her husband and recounts that she 'just lost her temper'. She describes that she 'let fly' at Ms McDonald but professes that at no time did she intend to inflict the serious injury caused (Ms McDonald had to have three stitches to repair her ear in the local hospital casualty department). Indeed, she describes that she was extremely shocked to find that there had been serious physical injury following her momentary loss of temper. She cannot understand how the damage was done in the two or three seconds of what she describes as a 'fight'.

Nevertheless, Mrs Smith realises that this is a very serious offence and she has expressed feelings of remorse for the pain that she has caused. When I visited her at her home she was extremely tearful in the interview. She wonders now if her anger wasn't misplaced to some extent since her husband was equally involved. I am told that the couple have begun to talk about their relationship more as a result of this incident. At the time, however, she tells me that she could think only of her love for him and she was afraid that she might lose him to Ms McDonald. She simply 'let fly' without thinking.

2. *Previous Offending*

There are no previous convictions, Mrs Smith being of previous good character.

3. *Relevant Family Background*

Jane Smith is the youngest of three children who grew up with their parents in Disset (near Edinburgh). She had a reasonably settled existence as a child until the age of 11 when her father went off with another woman and her mother was left to bring up the three children (all of school age at this time) on her own. Mrs Smith tells me that the family was pretty hard up from this point on because her father had been the main provider. Her mother went out to work as a result of his leaving, but she remembers that they had to scrimp and save for new clothes and that there were no holidays or extra treats from this point. She tells me that she was very often left to her own devices after school, but that on the whole her mother cared for the children as best she could in the circumstances. She has had no contact with her father since he left.

4. *Current Circumstances*

Jane Smith has no money or savings of her own. She and her husband bought their former council house in 1989 and now have negative equity of about £15,000. Since her husband works long hours as a bus driver in order to provide for the family and in order to pay off debts (to the tune of £2,000) resulting from hire purchase agreements when they purchased new furniture for their home in 1990, Mrs Smith finds that her time is fully occupied in caring for the children (aged seven, six and five). All three children are now at school, but Mrs Smith tells me that she spends much of the day taking and fetching them from the school which is at some distance from their home.

The family income is £16,000 per year. Out of a monthly income of £900 they pay £250 towards their mortgage, £200 a month on bills (electricity, gas and water rates) and a further sum on council tax charges. They pay £20 a month towards a clothing club. There are sums owing for furniture as described above. The remaining amounts are spent on food and household items. Mr Smith runs a moped to get himself to and from work.

Mrs Smith's mother, brother and sister live some 400 miles away in

Edinburgh, whilst Mr Smith's parents have both died.

5. *Conclusion*

In my view, Mrs Smith is clearly very shaken by this whole incident. She claims that she did not intend the injury and she is very sorry for the trouble she has caused.

This appears to be an offence which is completely out of character. Mrs Smith gives every impression of being a caring mother committed to their children. She is also devoted to her husband and appears to have acted spontaneously (if extremely foolishly) to protect their relationship. She did not raise the point herself, but it may be that her father's own departure for another woman contributed to the offence. The offence is obviously inexcusable, however, and Mrs Smith appreciates that she is in a very serious position before the court today.

In terms of suitable community penalties it seems to me that a lengthy Community Service Order would both mark the seriousness of the offence and be an important reminder of the need to think about the consequences of actions. Mrs Smith has met with the local Community Service Organiser and has been assessed as being suitable for community service. I am told that there would be a place available for her to work in a closely supervised team of offenders in a local authority old people's home. Child care arrangements will be difficult to manage alongside the working arrangements required by the such an order, but not impossible. The difficulties created will add to the penalty and serve to remind Mrs Smith that the loss of self-control always has serious consequences.

If the court is minded to impose a custodial sentence for the offence it is likely that Mr Smith would have to give up his job to care for the children. The only alternative would be for the children to be taken into care.

Angelita Margaret Blenkinsop
Probation Officer

Pre-sentence report on Jason Brown

Age :   24   D.O.B: 1.6.71

Address: 37, Kerridge Close

             Bolderton, Newark,

             Borcetshire

Offences: Affray, assault occasioning actual bodily harm

For the purposes of this report I have interviewed the defendant on one occasion in the Probation Office.

1. *Offence*

Jason Brown has pleaded guilty to one offence of affray and one of assault occasioning actual bodily harm.   Jason says that he was a passenger in his friend's car when another car tried to overtake them at some traffic lights. His friend indicated his annoyance to the people in the other car, at which the driver made a gesture at him which he interpreted as being obscene. The two cars pulled across the junction, Jason got out of the passenger door, ran round to the offside of the other car and punched the driver a few times on the side of the head.   Mr Brown admits that he had been drinking quite heavily on the afternoon prior to the incident.

2. *Previous Offending*

Jason Brown has four previous convictions, all for burglary. He has no previous conviction for any offence involving violence. He has in the past satisfactorily completed a community service order and a suspended sentence.

3. *Relevant Family Background*

Jason Brown is the younger of two brothers who grew up with their parents in the Walton area of Liverpool.   He attended a comprehensive school, leaving at sixteen with two passes at GCSE level. He has had a series of unskilled jobs interspersed with periods of unemployment.

4. *Current Circumstances*

He is at present living in rented accommodation and is at present unemployed, living on benefits. He has no savings.

5. *Conclusion*

Mr Brown claims that he does not have a drink problem and that he is not normally prone to violence.   He says that he acted in the way he did simply out of loyalty to a friend, who had stood up for him in the past. He has been assessed as being suitable for community service and work is available for him on a project involving manual labouring.

Alan Jackson,
Probation Officer

References

Barker, M. (1993) *Community Service and Women Offenders.* London: ACOP.

Caddle, D. and Crisp, D. (1997) *Mothers in Prison.* Research Findings No 38. London: Home Office.

Carlen, P. (1976) *Magistrates' Justice.* Oxford: Martin Robertson.

Carlen, P. (1988) *Women, Crime and Poverty.* Milton Keynes: Open University Press.

Daly, K. (1994) *Gender, Crime and Punishment,* New Haven, Connecticut: Yale University Press.

Datesman, S. and Scarpetti, F. (1980) *'Unequal protection for males and females in juvenile court'* in Datesman, S. and Scarpetti, F. (eds) *Women, Crime and Justice.* Oxford: Oxford University Press.

Eaton, M. (1983) *'Mitigating circumstances: familiar rhetoric',* International Journal of the Sociology of Law, 11, 385-400.

Eaton, M. (1986) *Justice for Women? Family, Court and Social Control.* Milton Keynes: Open University.

Edwards, S. S. M. (1984) *Women on Trial.* Manchester: Manchester University Press.

Efran, M.G. (1974) *'The effect of physical appearance on the judgement of guilt, interpersonal attraction and seventy of recommended punishment in a simulated jury task',* Journal of Research in Personality, 8, 45-54.

Farrington, D. P. and Morris, A. M. (1983) *'Sex, sentencing and reconviction',* British Journal of Criminology, 23, 229-48.

Gibson, B. and Cavadino, P (1995) *Introduction to the criminal justice process.* Winchester: Waterside Press.

Graham, J. and Bowling, B. (1995) *Young People and Crime*. Home Office Research Study 145. London: Home Office.

Green, P., Mills, C. and Read, T. (1994) *The characteristics and sentencing of illegal drug importers,* British Journal of Criminology, Vol. 34, No. 4, 479-486.

Hair, J. F., Anderson, R. E. and Tatham, R. L. (1987) *Multivariate Data Analysis with Readings.* New York: Macmillan.

Harvey, L., Burnham, R. W., Kendall, K. and Pease, K. (1992) *'Gender differences in criminal justice: an international comparison',* British Journal of Criminology, Vol. 32, No. 2, 208-217.

Hedderman, C. (1990) *'The effect of defendants' demeanour on sentencing in magistrates' courts',* Home Office Research Bulletin. No. 29.

Hedderman, C. and Hough, M. (1994) *Does the criminal justice system treat men and women differently?* Research Findings No. 10. London: Home Office.

Her Majesty's Inspectorate of Probation (1996) *A review of probation service provision for women offenders.* London: Home Office.

Hood, R. (1992) *Race and Sentencing: A study in the Crown Court.* Oxford: Clarendon Press.

Home Office (annually), *Criminal Statistics England and Wales.* London: HMSO.

Home Office (1994), *The Offenders Index: A short guide to the Offenders Index and its uses. Fourth edition July 1994,* Research and Statistics Department.

Home Office (1995) *National Standards for the supervision of offenders in the community.* London: Home Office, Department of Health, and Welsh Office.

Hough, M. (1996) *'People talking about punishment',* Howard Journal, Vol 35. No 3, 191-214.

Kapardis, A. and Farrington, D. P. (1981) *'An experimental study of sentencing by magistrates',* Law and Human Behaviour, 5, 107-121.

Morris A., Wilkinson C., Tisi, A., Woodrow, J. and Rockley A. (1995) *Managing the needs of women prisoners.* London: Home Office.

Moxon, D. (1988) *Sentencing Practice in the Crown Court.* Home Office Research Study No. 103. London: HMSO.

Moxon, D., Hedderman, C. and Sutton, M. (1990) *Deductions from benefit for fine default.* Research and Planning Unit Paper No. 60. London: Home Office.

Moxon, D., Corkery, J. and Hedderman, C. (1992) *Developments in the Use of Compensation Orders in Magistrates' courts since October 1988.* Home Office Research Study No. 126. London: HMSO.

NACRO (1991) *A Fresh Start for Women.* NACRO: London.

Norusis, M. J. (1993) *SPSS for Windows Advanced Statistics Release* 6.0. Chicago. SPSS INC.

Pearson, R. (1976) 'Women defendants in magistrates' courts', British Journal of Law and Society, 3, 265-273.

Rock, P (1993) *The social world of an English Crown Court: witness and professionals in the Crown Court Centre at Wood Green.* Oxford: Clarendon.

Seear, N. and Player, E. (1986) *Women and the Penal System.* London: Howard League.

Vennard, J. (1980) *Contested trials in magistrates' courts: the case for the Prosecution.* London: HMSO.

Wasik, M (1993) *Emmins on Sentencing.* London: Blackstone Press.

Worrall, A. (1987) '*Sisters in Law? Women defendants and women magistrates*' in Carlen, P. and (eds) *Gender, Crime and Justice.* Milton Keynes: Open University Press.

Worrall, A. (1990) *Offending women: female law breakers and the criminal justice system.* London: Routledge.

Yllö K. (1993) 'Through a Feminist lens: gender, power and violence' in *Current controversies on family violence,* (eds) Gelles, R.J. and Loseke D.R. London: Sage.

Young, W. (1979) *Community Sentence Orders: the development and use of a new penal measure.* Cambridge Studies in Criminology No. XLII. London: Heinemann.

Publications

List of research publications

A list of research reports for the last three years is provided below. A **full** list of publications is available on request from the Research and Statistics Directorate Information and Publications Group.

Home Office Research Studies (HORS)

133. **Intensive Probation in England and Wales: an evaluation.** George Mair, Charles Lloyd, Claire Nee and Rae Sibbett. 1994. xiv + 143pp. (0 11 341114 6).

134. **Contacts between Police and Public: findings from the 1992 British Crime Survey.** Wesley G Skogan. 1995. ix + 93pp. (0 11 341115 4).

135. **Policing low-level disorder: Police use of Section 5 of the Public Order Act 1986.** David Brown and Tom Ellis. 1994. ix + 69pp. (0 11 341116 2).

136. **Explaining reconviction rates: A critical analysis.** Charles Lloyd, George Mair and Mike Hough. 1995. xiv + 103pp. (0 11 341117 0).

137. **Case Screening by the Crown Prosecution Service: How and why cases are terminated.** Debbie Crisp and David Moxon. 1995. viii + 66pp. (0 11 341137 5).

138. **Public Interest Case Assessment Schemes.** Debbie Crisp, Claire Whittaker and Jessica Harris. 1995. x + 58pp. (0 11 341139 1).

139. **Policing domestic violence in the 1990s.** Sharon Grace. 1995. x + 74pp. (0 11 341140 5).

140. **Young people, victimisation and the police: British Crime Survey findings on experiences and attitudes of 12 to 15 year olds.** Natalie Aye Maung. 1995. xii + 140pp. (0 11 341150 2).

141. **The Settlement of refugees in Britain.** Jenny Carey-Wood, Karen Duke, Valerie Karn and Tony Marshall. 1995. xii + 133pp. (0 11 341145 6).

142. **Vietnamese Refugees since 1982.** Karen Duke and Tony Marshall. 1995. x + 62pp. (0 11 341147 2).

143. **The Parish Special Constables Scheme.** Peter Southgate, Tom Bucke and Carole Byron. 1995. x + 59pp. (1 85893 458 3).

144. **Measuring the Satisfaction of the Courts with the Probation Service.** Chris May. 1995. x + 76pp. (1 85893 483 4).

145. **Young people and crime.** John Graham and Benjamin Bowling. 1995. xv + 142pp. (1 85893 551 2).

146. **Crime against retail and manufacturing premises: findings from the 1994 Commercial Victimisation Survey.** Catriona Mirrlees-Black and Alec Ross. 1995. xi + 110pp. (1 85893 554 7).

147. **Anxiety about crime: findings from the 1994 British Crime Survey.** Michael Hough. 1995. viii + 92pp. (1 85893 553 9).

148. **The ILPS Methadone Prescribing Project.** Rae Sibbitt. 1996. viii + 69pp. (1 85893 485 0).

149. **To scare straight or educate? The British experience of day visits to prison for young people.** Charles Lloyd. 1996. xi + 60pp. (1 85893 570 9).

150. **Predicting reoffending for Discretionary Conditional Release.** John B Copas, Peter Marshall and Roger Tarling. 1996. vii + 49pp. (1 85893 576 8).

151. **Drug misuse declared: results of the 1994 British Crime Survey.** Malcom Ramsay and Andrew Percy. 1996. xv + 131pp. (1 85893 628 4).

152. **An Evaluation of the Introduction and Operation of the Youth Court.** David O'Mahony and Kevin Haines. 1996. viii + 70pp. (1 85893 579 2).

153. **Fitting supervision to offenders: assessment and allocation decisions in the Probation Service.** Ros Burnett. 1996. xi + 99pp. (1 85893 599 7).

154   **Ethnic minorities: victimisation and racial harassment. Findings from the 1988 and 1992 British Crime Surveys.** Marian Fitzgerald and Chris Hale. 1996. xi + 97pp (1 85893 603 9).

155   **PACE ten years on: a review of research.** David Brown. 1997. xx + 281pp. (1 85893 603 9).

156.   **Automatic Conditional Release: the first two years.** Mike Maguire, Brigitte Perroud and Peter Raynor. 1996. x + 114pp. (1 85893 659 4).

157.   **Testing obscenity: an international comparison of laws and controls relating to obscene material.** Sharon Grace. 1996. ix + 46pp. (1 85893 672 1).

158.   **Enforcing community sentences: supervisors' perspectives on ensuring compliance and dealing with breach.** Tom Ellis, Carol Hedderman and Ed Mortimer. 1996. x + 81pp. (1 85893 691 8).

160.   **Implementing crime prevention schemes in a multi-agency setting: aspects of process in the Safer Cities programme.** Mike Sutton. 1996. x + 53pp. (1 85893 691 8)

161.   **Reducing criminality among young people: a sample of relevant programmes in the United Kingdom.** David Utting. 1997. vi + 122pp. (1 85893 744 2).

162   **Imprisoned women and mothers.** Dianne Caddle and Debbie Crisp. 1996. xiii + 74pp. (1 85893 760 4)

163.   **Curfew orders with electronic monitoring: an evaluation of the first twelve months of the trials in Greater Manchester, Norfolk and Berkshire, 1995 - 1996.** George Mair and Ed Mortimer. 1996. x + 50pp. (1 85893 765 5).

165.   **Enforcing financial penalties.** Claire Whittaker and Alan Mackie. 1997. xii + 58pp. (1 85893 786 8).

166.   **Assessing offenders' needs: assessment scales for the probation service.** Rosumund Aubrey and Michael Hough. x + 55pp.(1 85893 799 X).

167.   **Offenders on probation.** George Mair and Chris May. 1997. xiv + 95pp. (1 85893 890 2).

168. **Managing courts effectively: The reasons for adjournments in magistrates' courts**. Claire Whittaker, Alan Mackie, Ruth Lewis and Nicola Ponikiewski. 1997. x + 37pp. (1 85893 804 X).

169. **Addressing the literacy needs of offenders under probation supervision.** Gwynn Davis et al. 1997. xiv + 109pp. (1 85893 889 9.

Nos 159, and 164 not published yet.

Research and Planning Unit Papers (RPUP)

86. **Drug Education Amongst Teenagers: a 1992 British Crime Survey Analysis**. Lizanne Dowds and Judith Redfern. 1995.

87. **Group 4 Prisoner Escort Service: a survey of customer satisfaction.** Claire Nee. 1994.

88. **Special Considerations: Issues for the Management and Organisation of the Volunteer Police.** Catriona Mirrlees-Black and Carole Byron. 1995.

89. **Self-reported drug misuse in England and Wales: findings from the 1992 British Crime Survey.** Joy Mott and Catriona Mirrlees-Black. 1995.

90. **Improving bail decisions: the bail process project, phase 1.** John Burrows, Paul Henderson and Patricia Morgan. 1995.

91. **Practitioners' views of the Criminal Justice Act: a survey of criminal justice agencies.** George Mair and Chris May. 1995.

92. **Obscene, threatening and other troublesome telephone calls to women in England and Wales: 1982-1992.** Wendy Buck, Michael Chatterton and Ken Pease. 1995.

93. **A survey of the prisoner escort and custody service provided by Group 4 and by Securicor Custodial Services.** Diane Caddle. 1995.

Research Findings

12. **Explaining Reconviction Rates: A Critical Analysis.** Charles Lloyd, George Mair and Mike Hough. 1995.

13.   **Equal opportunities and the Fire Service.** Tom Bucke. 1994.

14.   **Trends in Crime: Findings from the 1994 British Crime Survey.**
Pat Mayhew, Catriona Mirrlees-Black and Natalie Aye Maung. 1994.

15.   **Intensive Probation in England and Wales: an evaluation.**
George Mair, Charles Lloyd, Claire Nee and Rae Sibbitt. 1995.

16.   **The settlement of refugees in Britain.** Jenny Carey-Wood,
Karen Duke, Valerie Karn and Tony Marshall. 1995.

17.   **Young people, victimisation and the police: British Crime Survey
findings on experiences and attitudes of 12- to 15- year-olds.**
Natalie Aye Maung. 1995.

18.   **Vietnamese Refugees since 1982.** Karen Duke and Tony Marshall.
1995.

19.   **Supervision of Restricted Patients in the Community.**
Suzanne Dell and Adrian Grounds. 1995.

20.   **Videotaping children's evidence: an evaluation.** Graham Davies,
Clare Wilson, Rebecca Mitchell and John Milsom. 1995

21.   **The mentally disordered and the police.** Graham Robertson,
Richard Pearson and Robert Gibb. 1995.

22.   **Preparing records of taped interviews.** Andrew Hooke and
Jim Knox. 1995.

23.   **Obscene, threatening and other troublesome telephone calls
to women: Findings from the British Crime Survey.**
Wendy Buck, Michael Chatterton and Ken Pease. 1995.

24.   **Young people and crime.** John Graham and Ben Bowling. 1995.

25.   **Anxiety about crime: Findings from the 1994 British Crime
Survey.** Michael Hough. 1995.

26.   **Crime against retail premises in 1993.** Catriona Mirrlees-Black
and Alec Ross. 1995.

27.   **Crime against manufacturing premises in 1993.**
Catriona Mirrlees-Black and Alec Ross. 1995.

28.   **Policing and the public: findings from the 1994 British Crime Survey.** Tom Bucke. 1995.

29.   **The Child Witness Pack – An Evaluation.** Joyce Plotnikoff and Richard Woolfson. 1995.

30.   **To scare straight or educate? The British experience of day visits to prison for young people.** Charles Lloyd. 1996.

31.   **The ADT drug treatment programme at HMP Downview – a preliminary evaluation.** Elaine Player and Carol Martin. 1996.

32.   **Wolds remand prison – an evaluation.** Keith Bottomley, Adrian James, Emma Clare and Alison Liebling. 1996.

33.   **Drug misuse declared: results of the 1994 British Crime Survey.** Malcolm Ramsay and Andrew Percy. 1996.

34.   **Crack cocaine and drugs-crime careers.** Howard Parker and Tim Bottomley. 1996.

35.   **Imprisonment for fine default.** David Moxon and Claire Whittaker. 1996.

36.   **Fine impositions and enforcement following the Criminal Justice Act 1993.** Elizabeth Charman, Bryan Gibson, Terry Honess and Rod Morgan. 1996.

37.   **Victimisation in prisons.** Ian O'Donnell and Kimmett Edgar. 1996.

38   **Mothers in prison.** Dianne Caddle and Debbie Crisp. 1997.

39.   **Ethnic minorities, victimisation and racial harassment.** Marian Fitzgerald and Chris Hale. 1996.

40.   **Evaluating joint performance management between the police and the Crown Prosecution Service.** Andrew Hooke, Jim Knox and David Portas. 1996.

41.   **Public attitudes to drug-related crime**. Sharon Grace. 1996.

42.   **Domestic burglary schemes in the safer cities programme**. Paul Ekblom, Ho Law and Mike Sutton. 1996.

43.   **Pakistani women's experience of domestic violence in Great Britain.** Salma Choudry. 1996.

44.   **Witnesses with learning disabilities**. Andrew Sanders, Jane Creaton, Sophia Bird and Leanne Weber. 1997.

45.   **Does treating sex offenders reduce reoffending?** Carol Hedderman and Darren sugg. 1996.

46.   **Re-education programmes for violent men - an evaluation.** Russell Dobash, Rebecca Emerson Dobash, Kate Cavanagh and Ruth Lewis. 1996.

47.   **Sentencing without a pre-sentence report**. Nigel Charles, Claire Whittaker and Caroline Ball. 1997.

48   **Magistrates' views of the probation service.** Chris May. 1997.

49.   **PACE ten years on: a review of the research**. David Brown. 1997.

53.   **A reconviction study of HMP Grendon Therapeutic Community.** Peter Marshall. 1997.

55.   The prevalence of convictions for sexual offending. Peter Marshall. 1997.

Nos 50 - 52 and 54 not yet published.

Research Bulletins (no longer produced)

The Research Bulletin contains short articles on research and back issues are still available.

Occasional Papers

Measurement of caseload weightings associated with the Children Act. Richard J. Gadsden and Graham J. Worsdale. 1994. (Available from the RSD Information and Publications Group).

Managing difficult prisoners: The Lincoln and Hull special units. Professor Keith Bottomley, Professor Norman Jepson, Mr Kenneth Elliott and Dr Jeremy Coid. 1994. (Available from the RSD Information and Publications Group).

The Nacro diversion initiative for mentally disturbed offenders: an account and an evaluation. Home Office, NACRO and Mental Health Foundation. 1994. (Available from the RSD Information and Publications Group.)

Probation Motor Projects in England and Wales. J P Martin and Douglas Martin. 1994.

Community-based treatment of sex offenders: an evaluation of seven treatment programmes. R Beckett, A Beech, D Fisher and A S Fordham. 1994.

Videotaping children's evidence: an evaluation. Graham Davies, Clare Wilson, Rebecca Mitchell and John Milsom. 1995.

Managing the needs of female prisoners. Allison Morris, Chris Wilkinson, Andrea Tisi, Jane Woodrow and Ann Rockley. 1995.

Local information points for volunteers. Michael Locke, Nick Richards, Lorraine Down, Jon Griffiths and Roger Worgan. 1995.

Mental disorder in remand prisoners. Anthony Maden, Caecilia J. A. Taylor, Deborah Brooke and John Gunn. 1996.

An evaluation of prison work and training. Frances Simon and Claire Corbett. 1996.

The Impact of the National Lottery on the Horse-Race Betting Levy. Simon Field. 1996.

Reviewing risk. A review of research on the assessment and management of risk and dangerousness: implications for policy and practice in the Probation Service. Hazel Kemshall. 1996. (available from IPG).

Crack cocaine and drugs - crime careers. Howard Parker and Tim Bottomley. 1996.

The social implications of casino gambling. Iain Brown and Sue Fisher (edited by Clem Henricson and Joel Miller). 1996.

Evaluation of a Home Office initiative to help offenders into employment. Ken Roberts, Alana Barton, Julian Buchanan and Barry Goldson. 1996.

Requests for Publications

Home Office Research Studies from 143 onwards, *Research and Planning Unit Papers, Research Findings and Research Bulletins* can be requested, **subject to availability,** from:

Research and Statistics Directorate
Information and Publications Group
Room 201, Home Office
50 Queen Anne's Gate
London SW1H 9AT
Telephone: 0171 273 2084
Fascimile: 0171 222 0211
Internet: http://www.open.gov.uk/home off/rsdhome.htp

Occasional Papers can be purchased from (unless otherwise otherwise):
Home Office
Publications Unit
50 Queen Anne's Gate
London SW1H 9A1
Telephone: 0171 273 2302

Home Office Research Studies prior to 143 can be purchased from:

HMSO Publications Centre

(Mail, fax and telephone orders only)
PO Box 276, London SW8 5DT
Telephone orders: 0171 873 9090
General enquiries: 0171-873 0011
(queuing system in operation for both numbers)
Fax orders: 0171-873 8200

And also from **HMSO Bookshops**